D1325625

SUN HORSE,
MOON HORSE

BY THE SAME AUTHOR

(published by The Bodley Head)

Beowulf : Dragon Slayer
The Hound of Ulster
The High Deeds of Finn Mac Cool
Tristan and Iseult

SUN HORSE, MOON HORSE

Rosemary Sutcliff

Decorations by
SHIRLEY FELTS

THE BODLEY HEAD
LONDON SYDNEY
TORONTO

This book is for
Anthony Kamm

© Rosemary Sutcliff 1977
Decorations © The Bodley Head 1977
ISBN 0 370 30048 3

Printed and bound in Great Britain for
The Bodley Head Ltd
9 Bow Street, London WC2E 7AL
by Cox & Wyman Ltd, Fakenham
Set in Monophoto Imprint 101
First published 1977

CONTENTS

AUTHOR'S NOTE

Most of the White Horses still to be seen cut on English hillsides have only been there since the eighteenth or even the nineteenth centuries; but the White Horse of Uffington, high on the Berkshire Downs, belongs to a much older world; nobody knows for sure how long ago it was made, but probably about a hundred years before the birth of Christ. And whereas the other horses stand stiff and still on their hillsides, elegant, sometimes, but without any spark of life, the Uffington White Horse is magical; full of movement and power and beauty.

I have always felt that anything so magical must have a story behind it. A long-forgotten story, which I should love to tell. And then one day, reading T. C. Lethbridge's book *Witches*, I came upon his theory that the Iceni, the great Early Iron Age tribe who inhabited East Anglia, were also in the Chilterns and the Down Country north of the Upper Thames Valley, until they were forced out by invaders from the south. And I began to get an idea of what the story might be.

Sun Horse, Moon Horse is the result.

Mr Lethbridge believes that the Iceni who were forced out became the Epidi of Argyll and Kintyre—Epidi and Iceni both mean "Horse People"—and if that is true, then it must mean that Lubrin's people got through safely to their new horse-runs in the north, and in a way my story has a happy ending.

If any of you who read it have already followed the adventures of Marcus and Esca in *The Eagle of the Ninth*, and think that Lubrin's people are not very like the Epidi who they found when they went north to rescue the eagle of the lost legion, I can only say that when I wrote *that* story, I had not read *Witches*. And if I had, I would have made them a slightly different people. Though, of course, they might have changed quite a lot in more than two hundred years.

SUN HORSE,
MOON HORSE

THE WHITE MARE
OF A DREAM

The dun, the Strong Place, crouched on the highest wave-lift of the Downs. Three encircling banks, one within the other, turf-built and timber-faced, and the broad chalk-cut ditch outside all. And where the gateways made weak places in the defences, the ends of the inner and outer banks were joined together, so that the heavy timber gates were set at the end of a kind of passage-way, and an attacking war-host could only reach them through a crossfire of spears and slingstones from the defenders on either side.

Five times the life of a man, the Strong Place had crouched there, ever since the young men of the tribe, following a queen's youngest son, had come thrusting along the Downs from the vast flat grasslands far to the north-east, to find new lands for themselves in the way of young men all the world over. They had brought their women and their children and their horse herds with them. They were of the Iceni, the Horse People, breeders and breakers of horses, counting their wealth not in gold, but in stallions and rough-coated two-year-olds and foaling mares, and trained chariot teams.

They had found their new horse-runs, here along the High Chalk, and driven out the Dark People, the Old People who had been there before them, and built their Strong Place; and in the early years, the whole clan had lived within the shelter of its ramparts. But now the Old People had settled into a life of their own in the shadow of the men who had once been their conquerors, and the times had become less fierce. In time of danger, under a raiding moon, the whole clan and the flower of the horse herds, sometimes even some of the Old People, too, could still refuge there, while the herdsmen drove the cattle and the rest of the horses off into the hidden places in the woods below. But in time of peace, most people lived in settlements along the lower and more sheltered slopes, or in clearings of the valley woods. And the smaller strongposts were used now as corrals for the autumn round-up or the mares at foaling time.

Only Tigernann the Chieftain still had his great timber hall up there on the windy roof of the world, with its byres and barns and stables gathered about it, and the lodgings of his household warriors, and his harper and his champion and his priests, and the craftsmen who made such things as a chieftain and his warriors and his horses need.

Tigernann the Chieftain had three sons born to

Saba his wife in the women's place behind the great hall, Brach and Corfil who were litter-brothers born at one birth, and Lubrin, the younger by two years. Lubrin Dhu, the little dark one, who came into the world with black down on his head, and eyes that seemed too old for his face from the moment he first opened them.

It happened so from time to time among the clan, for there was never a conquering people yet who did not mingle their blood a little with the people who were before them. And Lubrin's mother wept when he was born, for it was through her that the darkness came, though herself she was creamy-skinned and copper-haired as any other woman of the Horse People, and she knew something of the joys and the sorrows and the dreams that would be part of him, and that the rest of his kind would never be troubled with nor understand.

But Lubrin Dhu was happy enough as the first years of his life went by, tumbling with the hound pups and the other children of the dun about the threshold of his father's hall.

One hot summer day when he was five years old, he was playing with a hound puppy in the stable court. After a while, the puppy grew tired of the game and wandered off about its own affairs. Lubrin remained where he was, sitting on his heels. In the quietness after the puppy's going, he had become aware of the swallows who had their nests under the eaves of the stable sheds.

They were darting low after the dancing midge cloud, sweeping and skimming, weaving their pattern of flight against the sky. It seemed to Lubrin that he

13

could see the pattern. But it changed so quickly. Something in him longed to capture it before it was lost. He began to draw with his fingers in the dust, trying to catch the dark sickle-flash of wings, almost as one might try to catch a living thing in one's hands. But they were too fast, too fast, and escaped him every time.

At the upper end of the court, Urien his father's charioteer had pulled down one of the light hunting chariots from where they stood tipped up against the chariot shed wall, and was backing the red pair under the yoke. They fidgeted and side-stepped, tossing their heads in the air and swishing their tails. Urien said, "Easy! Easy now, my brothers! Have you never smelled thunder in the air before?"

In the usual way of things, Lubrin would have been with them, watching—as close as he dared, for Urien did not care for children underfoot when he was dealing with a nervous team—for he loved his father's chariot ponies, the red team best of all. But he was still too caught up in the darting and swooping and swerving of the swallows overhead, and his own efforts to catch the pattern they made before it was lost in the blue air. He did not even notice when Tigernann his father came into the stable court, and sprang up into the chariot, taking the reins from his waiting charioteer, and turned the red team towards the gateway. Lubrin Dhu had had an idea.

Somebody, bringing up branches for bedding from the woods below, had dropped a slender spray of birch. It lay in the white dust close beside him, three of the leaves on it already touched with gold. If he singled out just one of the darting swallows and ran after it very fast, following every twist and turn, and dragging the birch spray behind him in the dust, and then did it again with another bird, and another—and another . . .

He caught up the birch spray and stood ready, staring upward. A swallow darted out from the eaves directly overhead, and he was off after it, darting and swerving, his face turned skyward, the birch spray bobbing behind him, but already the swallow, his swallow, was gone, lost among a cloud of crescent wings.

And in its place there were ponies' upflung heads; open mouths and snorting nostrils, a tossing tangle of fiery manes. Hooves seemed crashing all around and over him. There was a moment of trampling chaos as the team were wrenched to one side and reined back on their haunches; and he was looking up over the wicker side of the chariot into his father's angry face.

"What in the name of Epona do you think that you are doing?" demanded Tigernann, quietening his startled beasts.

Lubrin stood his ground and looked back into the gathering storm between the Chieftain's brows. Something within him knew that it was going to be too complicated to explain that he had been trying to catch the pattern of the swallows' flight. "I was being a swallow," he said.

"It is in my mind that you came near to being a dead swallow. Also you have startled my horses."

The charioteer had come running to scoop Lubrin out of the way, but Tigernann gestured him back.

Lubrin said nothing. There did not seem anything to say. He and his father went on looking at each other.

15

Until now, Lubrin Dhu had not been much aware of his father, save as something large and strong and splendid and terrifying, a sort of combined sunburst and thundercloud, on the edge of his world. Now, meeting the angry blue gaze, he discovered for the first time that Tigernann the Chieftain was indeed his father, and a man like other men. It was a discovery that felt good in the making. And at the same time, Tigernann was making much the same kind of discovery. It was the first time since he was born that the Chieftain had really looked with a seeing eye at his third son; the little black runt of a golden litter. But he was seeing him now, and suddenly his heart warmed to what he saw. He liked this creature, who had not made any outcry when he found himself almost under the ponies' hooves, this creature who stood scarcely higher than the rim of his chariot wheel, and was not afraid of him but gave him back look for look.

"Come," he said, on an impulse, "we are not Bird People, we are Horse People, you and I. Come with me and see the mares in the High Run."

And before Lubrin knew what was happening, his father had stooped and caught him up into the chariot beside him, and the team sprang forward from a flick of the reins.

They clattered out through the eastward gate of the dun, and swung aside on to the track that crested the long ridge of the Chalk. And Tigernann let out his whip lash, flickering and cracking above the backs of the red team, as they sprang forward into full gallop.

To their right, as they left the great up-rearing of the Fortress Hill behind them, the land fell away gently, past the barley strips of the lower slopes already whitening towards harvest, to the dim far-off blueness of lowland forest. To their left, the northern side, it swooped and plunged in whirlpools of headlong turf to the nearer woods. And between the two, high up with the sun and the clouds and the larks for company, they followed the crest of the Chalk.

They were out now, from the thickets of bramble and wayfaring trees and the quiet grave mounds that marked the track, onto the open ground south of it. The red team were going full stretch; the turf, thin and tawny with late summer, streaked backwards beneath them, and the world was full of the thunder of hooves and iron-shod wheels. Lubrin felt the woven leather straps of the chariot floor vibrating under him. The chariot leapt and rocked, and he gave up trying to steady himself by the side, and clung instead to one of his father's wide-planted legs, because that seemed the surest thing to cling to. His brothers Brach and Corfil would have lifted up their voices, singing and shouting to the wind of their going; but Lubrin was silent; and his father looked down, half scornfully, to see if he was frightened, and saw that he was not, but that the shouting and singing were all within him.

That day, for the first time, Lubrin saw the herdsmen working the great horse herds, shifting them from one pasture to another for the late summer grazing. And he had never been so far from home before; and he had discovered that his father was real. And any of those things would have been enough to remember one day by. But he remembered it all his life as the day on which he saw the white mare.

There had been thunder muttering in the distance all day; one of those late summer days of quickly changing lights. And the smell of thunder was in the little puffs of warm wind that stirred the grass and the low-growing thorn scrub. And what he saw at first was a knot of mares heading at an easy canter along the ridge, the sky behind them massed with storm clouds that had the colour and bloom of ripe sloes, while the nearer slopes of turf were still in acid sunlight.

Then out from the rest, one took the lead, mane streaming, tail streaming, white against the gathering storm, whiter than the secret chalk below the grass, whiter than thorn blossom. For a few heartbeats of time she was his to see, with the skein of darker mares following after. And then, from out of the heart of the piled clouds, came a licking tongue of lightning. For an instant the mare seemed made of white fire, and the fire of her burned into the inmost self of the Chieftain's youngest son as a brand burns into the hide of a yearling colt, leaving a mark which is never quite lost.

Then she flung round, snorting with fear, and was gone over the lip of the Downs, the rest after her. And in the same instant, there was a crack of thunder like a whiplash, that turned into the roar of the skies falling, and boomed and echoed away among the combes and hollows of the Chalk. And Lubrin's father flung a dark wing of his cloak over him as the rain came hissing towards them along the dry ground.

Later, the sun came out again and everything was shining. But that was not what Lubrin remembered. He remembered the white mare, the dream.

2
FIGHT IN HALL

On the edge of autumn, Lubrin's sister was born. The priest-kind sounded the Moon Call on the sacred ox-horns that sent the news booming all along the run of the Downs. And that night there was a great feast in the Chieftain's hall.

It was a fine thing to have sons, but among Lubrin's people, kingship and chieftainship did not pass down from father to son, but were carried down by the daughters to the men they married. Tigernann was Chieftain because he was married to the old Chief's daughter, the Woman of the Clan. Now he had a daughter of his own, and so his line would carry on the chieftainship after him; and the clan feasted accordingly.

On any other night, Lubrin would have been curled

up in his sleeping rug of dappled faun skins in the women's quarters before the eating and drinking started. But this was not like other nights, and the women were busy about other things; and he and most of the children of the dun were with the hunting-dogs under the tables. When the warriors threw down bones and scraps of meat to the hounds, the children got their share; and Lubrin was more blissfully full of pig-meat and honey-baked badger than ever he had been before.

There had been much noisy drinking to the new daughter, and to the unknown warrior who would one day be her lord. "May he be such a one as led the clan from the eastern horse-runs!" the household warriors had shouted, gulping down the dark Greek wine that was too costly to be drunk except in time of high festival. But they had fallen quiet now, and Sinnoch the Chieftain's harper, sitting on his stool at the head of the long hearth, had begun to tune his little black bog-oak harp, gentling it into wakefulness as a man makes ready his hawk to fly. Then he tilted back his head and began to sing. He sang the old song of the droving, about the young men of the tribe who had followed a queen's youngest son out of the eastern grasslands to find new horse-runs in the morning time of the world.

> "Now," said the Youngest Son, "let us take the
>   horse herds, high crested and of fiery heart,
> And let us set our faces toward the West,
> Toward the land of the trees of silver apples.
>   Come!"
> And the hills trembled beneath the thunder of
>   their hooves,

And the dust-cloud of their chariot wheels rose
    to the sun.

Lubrin Dhu, under the high table, saw the firelight
leaping on the plucked harpstrings; but he was watch-
ing the pattern that the words and music had begun
to weave inside his head; deep strong flowing patterns
that had in them the beat of hooves and the streaming
of manes, and above and around the horse patterns,
the grace-notes rising like spun clouds, like flocks of
little birds wheeling and skimming above the herd.
And as he watched, the longing that he had had to
capture the swallows' flight came back on him again.

Scarcely knowing that he did so, he edged forward,
out from under the table, over the bracken-strewn
floor towards the bare flagstones that edged the
hearth. A piece of charred stick had fallen from the
fire; and he picked it up and began to draw on the
stone the thing that he was seeing inside his head. He
was so taken up with trying to catch the shapes as
they changed and flew that, just as he had done in the
stable court, he lost all awareness of what was around
him. The long timber hall, the warriors at the tables
and the women moving among them with the slender-
necked bronze wine jars; the firelight springing up
all the height of the roof trees, to where the skulls of
ancient enemies, smoke-blackened and daubed with
red and yellow ochre, were ranged along the tie-
beams overhead, all faded as into the dust-cloud of
the droving. And along with all else, he forgot about
the other children under the high table.

The pattern was coming. Anyone else might have
seen on the flagstone only a tangle of wavy lines and

random spots and dashes, but to Lubrin, coming closer to the secret of the thing this time than he had done with the swallows, it meant what he wanted it to mean, and it was beautiful; also, in a strange sort of way, it was part of himself.

And then suddenly Brach and Corfil, who had been tustling over a honeycake nearby, saw that he was doing something with a bit of charred stick on the hearthstone, and craned over to look. Corfil laughed. He had a wide scornful laugh that let you see right past where some of his cub teeth were missing, and down his pink throat. Then he got up, and deliberately walked across Lubrin's drawing, scuffing his feet as he went, so that the middle of it was all blurred and spoiled.

Brach, who always did what his twin did, would have followed him; but on the instant a red flower of rage seemed to burst open in Lubrin Dhu, and with a cry of fury he flung himself on Corfil, taking him by surprise so that he went over backwards, his mouth still open, but the laughter changed to blank astonishment. Brach dived in to his twin's aid. They had Lubrin between them, and pulled him down and hurled themselves upon him, pummelling and kicking. They were two to one, and Lubrin was two years younger, and small at that; but he fought like a wild thing cornered. Corfil yelped, and backed off for an instant with a bitten thumb, then came boring in again in a flailing mass of arms and legs.

But almost in the same instant a fourth-comer hurled himself into the fight, Dara, whose father Drochmail was chief among the household warriors, butting head down into Brach's belly.

Sinnoch had let his harp fall silent almost between note and note, and sat looking down with interest at the furious tangle that was rolling to and fro at his feet, almost in the ashes of the fire. Then two of the armour-bearers went in to break it up, as men go in half-laughing and dealing out cuffs right and left, to break up a fight among hound puppies.

And the thing was over. Lubrin's red rage-flower died, and he was standing in the grip of a young warrior, panting and still half-sobbing with rage and grief. But they were dry sobs, strangled in his chest. He would not weep like a child before the warriors of the clan. Above all, he would not weep before his brothers.

"And for what cause is all this snapping and snarling of whelps?" demanded Tigernann the Chief.

For a long breath of time, no one spoke. Then Brach said, "Ask Lubrin, my father. It was he that was the starting of it."

The Chief's golden brows twitched upward, as he turned to his youngest son. "Lubrin?"

Lubrin did not answer. He had known that it would be useless to try explaining to his father, when he had been trying to capture the swallows' flight. This would be still worse. If he said, "I was making a picture of Sinnoch's harpsong, and Corfil broke it," who would understand? He was not even sure that he understood himself, now that the thing was over and the magic broken.

"I am waiting, and I do not like to wait," said the Chieftain.

Lubrin shook his head. "I have forgotten," he said sullenly.

23

"So? And for a thing so small that you have forgotten it already, you will start a dogfight in the high hall?"

"Yes," said Lubrin.

They looked at each other as they had done across the chariot rim that time before. Then Tigernann leaned back in his seat with its covering of black ox-hides. "Then we will agree that it is finished for this time. But the next time, you will go outside to finish it in the forecourt, all of you; and the places where your tails would be, if you were whelps indeed, will be fiery behind you!"

The young warrior who had Lubrin by the back of the neck gave him a little shake, friendliwise, and let him go. Sinnoch's hand had begun to move once more on the strings of his harp, making again the shining sounds. His old faded gaze caught the small bright eyes of Gault the Bronzesmith, whose wonderful encircling patterns on a cup or a shield-boss seemed to hold the secrets of wind and stars and running water. They knew the meaning of the spoiled and half-rubbed-out lines on the hearthstone, and said to each other without words, "Here is another of the brotherhood."

But Lubrin saw nothing of that. He was looking at Dara; and Dara was licking a cut lip and looking back at him with round puzzled eyes.

Dara had not understood, any more than Corfil or Brach, but he had come to Lubrin's help without understanding. There were things happening inside both of them that they were not old enough to put into thought. They had played and fought together ever since they could crawl, along with all the young of the dun, human and hound pups alike, but it was not until that moment that they knew, far down below the need for thinking about it, that they were friends.

Lubrin grinned at Dara, and Dara grinned back, carefully, because it hurt where he had had somebody's heel driven into his mouth. And they retired companionably under the table once more, and squatted down with one of the hound puppies between them, and began to go over it for cockle burrs tangled in its rough coat.

And over their heads, the feasting and rejoicing continued, for the birth of the girl-child who would carry on the life of the clan.

3
MERCHANTS' TALES

The life of the clan went on; and the years turned full circle after each other. The mares dropped their foals in early summer, and in autumn the herds were rounded up for branding, and in winter the leggy two-year-olds began their breaking to rider or chariot.

And from the day of the fight at the girl-child, Teleri's, birth feast Lubrin and Dara held together. They were an oddly matched pair, especially as they grew older; Dara big-boned and golden-freckled and rangy as a wolfhound; little dark silent Lubrin beside him like his short noonday shadow. But in truth, Lubrin Dhu was nobody's shadow.

"They were born in the same moon. They are the two halves of a hazel-nut," said Sinnoch the Harper. "It is as simple as that."

So they hunted and laughed and fought together, shared their food from the same bowl and slept under the same rug most nights, until they were nine years old, and it was time for them to enter the Boys' House.

Every spring, on the day after the Beltane fires had burned out, the boys of the clan who had turned nine since last Beltane entered the Boys' House, the long low building at the lower end of the Chieftain's fore-court, to begin their warrior training. There were many things that they must learn and skills that they must master; skills of the war spear and the horse herd and the hunting trail. They had to learn the use of sword and spear and sling; how to kill and how to suffer pain with a shut mouth. They had to learn how to keep a whole herd on the move, and cut out a single colt for branding from among a flying cloud of year-lings. They had to learn how to build a chariot, for every one of the Men's Side must serve as a charioteer in his early years before he became a chariot-warrior himself, and every charioteer must be able to mend or replace the worn or broken parts of the chariot he drove. They must be able to break and train a chariot team as well as drive it. They must learn from the priest, Ishtoreth of the Oak, how to read and write the word-magic cut on peeled willow rods; and from Sinnoch they must learn by heart the songs that held within them the history of their people. And all these

27

things and many more they must master in just seven years.

"It is hard work, this training to be a man!" said Bryn, the biggest and strongest of them all, who liked to sleep in the sun.

Lubrin did not mind the hard work, but in the early years he minded very much the never being alone. The life of the Boys' House was close-knit, and the boys of each year worked together and slept close-huddled in their own part of the long building, and even in their spare time they mostly ran as a pack. Dara seemed quite happy with that way of things. But then, Dara did not have this aching need to catch and set down bird flight or harpsong, wind in barley or running herds. Nobody laughed at Dara or tormented him for the making of strange patterns. They laughed at Lubrin, led by Brach and Corfil who always laughed at anything they did not understand, in case, if they did not laugh, they might be afraid of it; and what was worse, they laughed at the picture-magics he made, so that for a long time he almost gave up making them except sometimes in secret. His refuge, during those years, was a great wych-elm on the edge of one of the forest clearings. He had found it before ever he went to the Boys' House, one day when he and Dara were hunting for a wild bees' nest. Three great limbs sprang from its main trunk, making it easy to climb, and up near the top it was antlered like a king stag, with a spreading poll of branches. He could lie up there above the tops of the lesser forest, secure from the rest of his world. Now and again, when the need to work out his strange patterns was sore upon him, he took a few bits of charred stick and a piece of silvery birch bark up with him—the deeply rutted grey bark of the tree was too rough to draw on —and made his private magic up there. There was even a deep crevice between two branches where he could hide his drawings for a while, until the weather got at them and fretted them away. At other times he went simply for the refuge, working his way far out along his favourite branch until it rose and fell under him with every movement of the wind. In a high wind it was like riding some giant unbroken horse; in gentle weather he could lie out along it half asleep in the dappled sunspots through the leaves, and look out southward to the great slow lift of the Downs rising to the Fortress Hill then sinking again on their way towards the sunset.

Lying up there one day he made the interesting discovery that if he shut one eye, he could cover the whole of his father's dun, the Boys' House and Brach and Corfil and the steep turf slopes below the ramparts and all, with a single elm leaf held before his face. It did not seem a very important discovery, but after he had made it, it ceased to matter so much when the others jeered at him and his picture-magic. "I can cover all of you with an elm leaf," he thought. And little by little, when they found that he did not mind any more, they mostly gave up jeering, and left him to be himself in his own way.

One day late in the third autumn that Lubrin and Dara spent in the Boys' House, a merchant came down the track from the north, with fine dressed skins in his ponies' packs, and ornaments of yellow Irish gold in a sealskin bag. Many merchants came and went through Tigernann's dun, for below its turf and timber walls the high Ridgeway and the way of the Horse People that shadowed it along the lower slopes crossed an ancient trade road running north and south. They were horse traders for the most part. Once, Tigernann's people, the Iceni, had bred their small fiery horses only for themselves, but now there were new markets for trained ponies opening in the south, and the traders came accordingly—but also dealers in skins from the north, and iron spear blades and dark salt from the rain forests far beyond the Great Water, and the bronze ingots that Gault and the smith-kind fashioned into fiercely beautiful wine-cups and war-caps and shield-bosses, and wine from the south in narrow-necked jars slung on either side of a pony's pack saddle.

And always it was the custom that the trader, when he had eaten in the Guest Place, should show his horses in the in-paddock, if he came to sell as well as buy, or spread his other wares before the High Seat in the hall, that the Chieftain, and after him his household warriors, might have first choice. And that next day he should show his wares in the open forecourt, that all who wished might come and do their bargaining. Then people would gather from far and wide, and not only to sell or buy, for beside their merchandise, the traders were the bearers of news, all the news of the world that they picked up on their travels and carried from place to place.

The Boys' House counted as part of the Chieftain's household, though only the boys in their last year ate in the hall with the warriors. And so that first evening, after the merchant had fed, those of them who had nothing more interesting to do went across to the

great timber hall to see what he had for sale and listen
to his stories. If they were lucky, he might be one of
those who are as full of travellers' tales as an egg is full
of meat, and anyway they would make a change from
the stories of Sinnoch the Harper, which everyone
knew by heart. It was good, sometimes, to hear a new
thing.

Lubrin was scratch-drawing the head of a hind on
a flat shoulderblade of the mutton they had had for
supper, trying to catch her in the instant before
flight, and he would have gone on drawing, leaving
the merchant's tales unheard, but Dara grabbed him
by the shoulder and hauled him to his feet. "She will
wait for you, and you can go on with her later," Dara
said, jerking his chin at the blade bone. Lubrin
doubted that. He doubted if he would be able to catch
the edge-of-flight moment again. But he went with
Dara and the rest, up past the tall black stone in the
centre of the forecourt, where the warriors sharpened
their weapons, to the open doorway of the hall.

In the smoky mingling of fire and torchlight the
Chieftain sat forward on his High Seat, watching as
the merchant brought out this thing and that from
his bale cloths and laid them on the piece of crimson
cloth spread at his feet. For the most part, the man
had left his furs in their bales—furs from the north
found a better market farther south—but he had
brought out some particularly fine marten pelts and
some beautifully marked mountain cat skins. They
lay on one side now, piled on the shaggy hide of a
brown bear, and the warriors and their women were
crowding close to look at the other things that he had
brought.

The boys edged through, getting as close as they could.

They saw a gold collar, and brooches set with red enamel that glowed like hot embers in the torchlight, and great arm-rings of gilded bronze, and a dagger whose hilt was shaped like a man with his arms folded across the top of his head. But the merchant himself, a dark, thickset man with black hairs curling on the backs of his forearms, seemed more akin to the piled furs than to the glinting gold and enamel and narwhal ivory that he handled as gently as a woman.

He had just tossed out on to the crimson cloth a jingle of small golden balls, each with a tiny loop to hang it by, and was picking them up again, delicately, casting two or three of them from hand to hand.

"And what are those?" the Chieftain said. "I have not seen their like before."

"Apples for a woman's hair. It is a new fashion among the fine ladies of Eriu. They plait their hair into many thin braids—ah, more than there are fingers on my two hands—and bind one of these to the end of each braid. A pretty fashion."

"Aye, a pretty fashion. From Eriu, you say? You are from Eriu, this time?"

"I was in Eriu earlier this summer. Why?"

The Chieftain shrugged. It was a small matter. "Traders from Eriu come almost always along the track from the west."

"I carried my trading up to the north of Eriu, and across to the Islands and so in to Albu. It was a new trail; and a trail that other men have not followed before is often good. But—" the merchant shook his head—"I would not follow it again. There are too few people between the mountains and the sea. Just sea-lakes and empty moors. For you, now, it would be a different creel of fish! An empty land, and wide grazing for the horse herds; good grazing in and out between the hazel woods and the heather . . ."

The young men looked at each other in the fire-light, and memory stirred in them, of Sinnoch's song of the Westward Droving. Lubrin could feel the stirring of it, the faint quickening in the blood, that leapt from one to another. His eyes met Dara's brightening gaze, and he saw that it was the same with him, too. In that moment, out of the merchant's random words and the memory of an old song, a dream was born between the two of them.

Then Tigernann turned to his wife, Lubrin's mother, sitting on piled deerskin cushions beside him. "Saba, my woman, how would it please you to dress your hair so?"

Saba shook her head. Her hair was gathered into an embroidered net, as many women of the Iceni wore it. "I am not wishing to change my own way for the fashion of the women of Eriu. If you would make me a gift, my lord, then let it be this," and she picked up a polished bronze mirror with blue and green enamel on the finely-chased back, and a handle of braided silver.

"It is your gift. It is for you to choose," Tigernann said; and to the merchant, "What will you take for the mirror?"

And while they fell to bargaining, Gault the Bronzesmith leaned forward, holding out his hand. "Lady, may I look?"

She gave it to him, and he sat turning it to the

light, tracing with his fingers the flowing lines, the three and fourfold curves that sprang from each other and curled back into each other again. And when the bargaining was over, he said to the merchant, "This is a good pattern. It would make a fitting pattern for a shield-boss." And gave Saba back her mirror.

The trader smiled. He had passed that way before, and he and Gault were well known to each other. "Is there anything in the world that you look at, without wondering will it make a fitting pattern for a shield-boss? And speaking of such matters, have you anything to show me if I come—humbly—to your workshop in the morning?"

"To show you, yes," Gault said. "Whether you would be wishing to buy, that is another thing; another thing altogether, and depends on who you would be wishing to sell to; my work does not speak to all men; and even for those it speaks to—it is not cheap."

"That, I know of old."

Gault smiled and spread his hands. "I have no need to sell cheaply."

"I can offer a good price," said the trader. "For it is in my mind that I can make a good sale. The Attribates are a rich people."

"The Attribates? So I have heard. Rich in those new gold coins that they have brought from Gaul. But surely they have bronzesmiths and shield-wrights of their own?"

"They are a great people, these chariot lords, and they have their bronzesmiths and their shield-wrights, fitting for their greatness. But in the way of

34

a rich people, above all a people rich in coins, which make for easy trading, they like to buy things strange to them, from outside their own workshops. Therefore they will pay."

In the little following silence, men glanced at each other. Then the Chieftain said, "I have heard something of these people who cross the Narrow Seas, to make their homes yonder." He jerked his thumb towards the great lowland forests to the south. "It is said that they come north, rather than lie themselves down on their bellies under the marching feet of the Red Crests. Well, that is a thing that we may all understand."

And they began to talk of the world beyond the Chalk and the forest, southward to the Great Water; and the heavy-handed people who called their war-hosts Legions, and marched in straight lines following gold and silver figures of their war gods in the shape of eagles, and wore crests of red horsehair on their helmets. The merchant had been amongst them more than once, and had wonderful stories to tell. And the others sat round listening. This was what they had really come for—the travellers' tales.

But Lubrin Dhu heard little of all that. He was still thinking about that country in the north. Empty horse-runs waiting, between the mountains and the sea. Dreaming foolish dreams to himself of the day when he and Dara would lead a new band of the young men north to find it. He saw the mares grazing under high mountains such as he had never seen waking in the daytime; and heard the harpers beside new hearths, making a new song of a new droving . . .

35

Dara was shaking him by the shoulder, and it was time to go back to the Boys' House.

That night he dreamed, as he had done time and again since he was five years old, of a white mare cantering along the ridge of the Downs, whiter than the secret chalk beneath the grass, whiter than thorn blossom, with the shadow-flow of the herd following after.

4
THE CHOOSING FEAST

The seven years of the Boys' House passed, and together with the rest of their year Lubrin and Dara went through the dark ceremonies of the Man-Making. Together they passed the Hidden Days; the three days when the women of the clan keened for them as for the dead. And together they came back, walking proud among the spear warriors, to their place in the Men's Side, with the newly-pricked and painted man-patterns still sore and reddened on their breasts and shoulders.

Now Lubrin wore the slim bronze collar that marked him, like Brach and Corfil, for a chief's son. But he and Dara were still, as old Sinnoch had said, "the two halves of a hazel-nut"; and still, though it had scarcely ever been spoken between them, they shared the dream of the horse-runs in the north.

Twice in every year, at the time of the Beltane fires, and again at Samhein for the autumn branding and the cattle slaughter, the herds were rounded up. And at about the start of the round-up the traders would begin to gather; and for a while the downland slopes around Tigernann's stronghold became a horse-fair. Both round-ups were a time for feasting after the day's work was over, and for the high ceremonies that helped the year to turn and the corn to ripen, the mares to drop many foals and the women to bear fine sons. But over the first Samhein gathering of Lubrin's manhood, there hung a dark shadow, for in the women's place behind the hall, Saba his mother, the Woman of the Clan, lay dying, wasted to a dry husk of herself, with some sickness deep within her that not all the healing skill of the priest-kind could set right.

The shadow lay cold between Lubrin and the sky. But the work of rounding up and branding must go on, and the Chieftain's sons must play their part in it. The cattle, like the sheep and the corn, were work for the Old People, but the horses were for the clansmen, and at Samhein and Beltane there was work for all, from the poorest warrior owning nothing but his spear to the Chief himself. Lubrin had been helping to herd a bunch of two-year-olds into the corral; and turning from heaving the gate-hurdle back into place, saw one of the strangers from the horse-fair leaning against the old turf wall and watching. A young man, short but strongly built; with a mane of straight fair hair, his eyes, as he studied the colts, making blue slits in his wind-burned face.

"These are a good batch," he said, looking round as though he felt Lubrin's gaze upon him.

Lubrin summed him up, taking in without quite knowing that he was doing so, something about the man's hands and the way he stood balanced on the balls of his feet. "I would be thinking the matched chariot teams had been more of interest to you."

The stranger smiled, showing strong crooked teeth. "The two-year-olds of this autumn are the matched chariot teams of two autumns' time. I like to see the raw material."

"Now I know you're a charioteer," Lubrin said. "As for the raw material, there's plenty more of that in the western run." He hesitated. "I am heading that way now, to bring in another batch. Will you ride with me?"

"I will so, and gladly," the other said, "if you can find me a horse. My own is back in the trade camp."

His hand already on the bridle of his own little dark mare, Lubrin called to a man passing by, and he brought up a sorrel with a striped riding blanket ready flung over its back; and a short while later the two of them were heading at a canter along the Downs south-westward. Ahead of them and to their left as they rode, the whole lie of the country dropped away gently to the wide wooded emptiness of the river lands. In clear weather you could see the far hills beyond, deep into Attribates territory. But today a faint autumn haze, blue as woodsmoke, hung over the lowlands, and all the country southward might have been the country of a dream; and out of the dream, the cloud shadows came drifting up over the bare, hound-tawny turf. Like great armies, Lubrin thought suddenly, like vast slow charges of shadow-chariots.

"You will have been among the Attribates?" he said, not quite knowing why.

"And in Gaul before that. Anywhere where there are horses to be bought and sold."

"They say that one day we shall have fighting."

"Fighting?" The stranger looked round at him quickly.

"That the Attribates will push forward again, to make a new frontier for their hunting runs." Lubrin was ashamed, even as he said it, of the chill that touched him at his own words. He was a warrior; he should be eager to blood his spear. "It's what they say," he added lamely.

"Who say?"

"The old men. As long as I can remember."

"The old men always say that, in all times, in all tribes. If they say it long enough, it comes to be true in the end."

"Maybe." Lubrin heeled his mare into a gallop, and swung away down into the long combe where the herdsmen were at their work, and the hill shoulder dappled with hawthorn scrub cut off the long view from the south, and the drifting cloud shadows.

When he rode back through the gates of the dun that evening, he heard the women keening, and knew that his mother was dead. And he thought no more of the stranger he had ridden with that day.

Lubrin's mother was laid in her sleeping place,

with her best blue glass necklace round her neck, and the bronze mirror with the silver handle beside her. And Lubrin cried for her going, all through one long rainy autumn night, as, almost seventeen years before, she had cried for him.

And life went on.

Now they must hold the Choosing Feast. Teleri was only just twelve, and in the usual way of things they would have waited until her fourteenth year, and held Choosing Feast and Marriage Feast within a few days of each other. But now that Saba her mother was dead, she was the Woman of the Clan, and no time must be lost in finding who among the young warriors was to be her lord, and lead the clan after Tigernann's time was done.

So the Feast was held, and the priest Ishtoreth of the Oak drank the Cup of Seeing, the bee beer in which certain herbs had been steeped to open the eyes of the spirit. Then he went down to the sheltered hollow in the Chalk where the nine sacred apple trees grew within their low turf walls, and lay down under the oldest apple tree and slept, that Epona, the Lady of the Foals, the Great Mother, might tell him in his sleep the name of the chosen warrior.

All that night, while Ishtoreth slept in the sacred place, muffled in his horse-skin robe against the thin scurrying rain, the feasting went on in the Chieftain's hall and forecourt. But with the first grey light of dawn, the feasting fell away, and men began to turn toward the west gate that had stood open all night long—and a great quietness of waiting spread over all the dun.

It was so quiet that when at last they heard slow

footsteps coming up the track, and the rattle of a scuffed pebble, the sounds seemed to fill the whole morning. And then Ishtoreth was standing on the broad threshold stone, with the ritual patterns on his skin blurred by the rain, and black hollows around his eyes, and the look on him of a man who has not slept at all, but is just returned from a long, long journey.

Utter silence still held the waiting dun. Lubrin, standing beside Dara among the young warriors, heard the whisper of the autumn rain and the thin wind soughing over the hilltop, and a horse stamping in the stable court.

Ishtoreth came slowly across the forecourt, through the open space that the crowd had fallen back to make for him, past the tall black weapon-stone, to where Tigernann waited for him on the threshold of the hall.

Tigernann spoke the ritual words. "Have you been? Have you seen? Have you asked the question? Do you bring the answer?"

Ishtoreth answered, scarcely louder than the faint wet soughing of the wind. "I have been. I have seen. I have asked the question and I bring the answer."

"Speak, then, for we have waited long."

Ishtoreth turned about beside the Chieftain, to face the crowded forecourt. Suddenly he raised his arms, and this time his voice sent the silence flying like a trumpet blast. "Hear and listen, oh, People of the Horse. For I, Ishtoreth have slept the Choosing Sleep, and spoken with Epona, the Lady of the Foals, mother of all things that be. And from her I bring the name of the warrior who shall be lord of the Woman of the Clan, and lord of all your spears when the strength fails from the spear arm of Tigernann!"

And again there was the waiting silence, and the little wind, and the horse stamping in the stable court.

Then the people cried out, "Speak the name, Ishtoreth Oak Priest!"

And yet again the silence, and again Ishtoreth sent it flying. "This name speaks the Mother, sitting beneath her apple trees with her mares grazing about her, and foals nuzzling apples from her lap. It is the name of Dara, son of Drochmail! He shall be lord to the Woman of the Clan, and lord of the clan when the time comes upon him."

And the Men's Side took up the shout, "Dara, son of Drochmail! Dara, son of Drochmail!"

Tigernann stepped forward. And Lubrin, with a small cold sense of unbelieving shock in his belly, felt Dara beside him check for an instant like a startled animal. Then the place beside him was empty, as his more-than-brother walked out to meet the Chieftain in the midst of the open space.

Dara took the Chieftain's hands between his own, and raised them to his forehead, while all the Men's Side shouted and beat the butts of their spears upon the ground until the Chalk seemed to give back a kind of throbbing underfoot, like the beat of a great sleeping heart deep down and far off.

That was when Lubrin slipped away by himself, out from the dun and down the broad dyke between the lower horse-runs, that served as a drove road at gathering times, to the valley woods. His feet took him without much help from his head, back to the great wych-elm on the edge of its clearing, that had so often been his refuge when the life of the Boys' House became too much for him. He climbed almost without thought, knowing the branch-way as a man knows the track to his own threshold; and soon he was lying out along his favourite branch. The leaves were almost all gone now, though below him the birch and hazel and oak scrub were still russet and gold with the shabby fires of autumn, the grey of the deeply crannied bark deepened almost to black by the rain. But the refuge was still there, just as it always had been. He did not look out, today, towards the dun crouching on its high lift of the Downs, his father's dun that he could cover with an elm leaf. He lay with his face pressed down on his forearm, staring into his own blackness. He didn't even think very much.

Oddly, he did think a little of Teleri, wondering how it would be with her when the word was brought to her in the women's quarters. He knew so little of her. She had been only four when he went to the Boys' House; a plump soft little creature, who cried when she did not get what she wanted from life. He wondered if she was crying now. Maybe she was glad. . . . He stopped thinking; just lay there for a long time, aware of the familiar living strength of the tree-branch under him, and staring into the dark.

A long while later he heard a faint brushing through the undergrowth below him, something, someone, coming along the edge of the clearing. He opened his eyes and looked down through the red-brown twig-tangle and saw that it was Dara.

He slipped off the branch, and hung, feeling with his toes for the branch below him; got another hand-hold and dropped again, swinging down from branch to branch, to make his final landing just as Dara reached the foot of the tree. It was better to come out of refuge to meet the Thing than to wait while the Thing came into refuge after you.

They stood and looked at each other, the hot blue eyes and the cool dark. And while they looked, a chill breath of edge-of-winter wind came siffling along the woodshore, scattering the wet from the grey thistle-heads and dead spires of last summer's foxgloves, and died away.

"I came to find you," Dara said at last, "it is time for more feasting."

And Lubrin realised that the light was beginning to fade.

"How did you know where to find me?" he asked.

"It's not so long since the Boys' House."

But his tree was the one thing he had never shared even with Dara.

Dara saw the look on his face, and answered it as though the words had been spoken. "There was the time you tore your new saffron kilt and left shreds of it hanging among the lower branches. A good thing it was I that saw them and not any of the others."

"Na, it would have been small matter who found them. I can outclimb any of you."

"Only because you are no bigger than a squirrel."

They laughed, trying, with easy insults, to catch back the old easy brotherhood; and the laughter died in their aching throats. Nothing could ever be quite the same again. They looked at each other, not speaking; and the dream died between them, the dream of the shared northward droving. If ever that happened, it must be for Lubrin alone to lead the young men to the new horse-runs. Dara could never leave the dun on the High Chalk, now.

They put their arms round each other for a moment, as though in farewell. And then Lubrin said, "Come then, we must go back to the feasting."

5
MENACE FROM
THE SOUTH

Almost two years must pass before the binding
together of Dara and Teleri could be made complete,
for no woman of the clan could go to a husband's
hearth until she was turned fourteen. So for almost
two years Teleri lived still as a daughter in the
women's quarters, and Dara spread his sleeping-rug
with the rest of the young warriors in the hall. And
on the surface, all was as it had been before Ishtoreth
slept the Choosing Sleep among the sacred apple
trees.

Twice more, snow lay over the Downs, and the
men of the clan turned out night after night, along
with the Old People, to keep the Wolf Guard. Twice
more, the turf grew dry and slippery in the summer
heat, and the south wind was full of the scent of

thyme and clover and the blue swaying scabious flowers. And the sheep lambed and the mares dropped their foals; and Lubrin's wych-elm budded into a smoke of tiny purplish flowers in the earliest spring.

And now it was not only the old men who spoke of war with the Attribates. Every merchant from the south brought tales of men furbishing their weapons; of new chariots being built and new teams trained; so that Tigernann gave orders for a constant watch to be kept along the southern runs of the Iceni. And they blocked up the eastern gate of the dun, and broke down the causeway on that side, so that if the attack came—when the attack came—there would be only one gateway to defend.

But the year turned again to harvest time, for all that, the barley white for the sickle along the slopes of the Downs. And with the first new moon after the harvest, the women already busy on the threshing-floors levelled out of the chalk, it was time for the Marriage Feast to be made for Dara and Teleri.

At first light on the day of the new moon, the clan began to gather; and all day the crowd grew thicker, as the people of the Iceni came flocking in from steadings and settlements among the lowland forest and across the High Chalk. Warriors in their finest cloaks riding their most fiery horses, and their women with the sacred vervain braided in their hair. Soon the dun was as thronged as a Beltane horse-fair, alive with voices and laughter, harpsong and the whinnying and stamping of horses; with the saffron and blue and crimson of fine clothes and the bronze glint of brooch and dagger, and the baking smell of whole carcases of deer and bullock and sheep from the cooking-pits.

But as the shadows lengthened towards evening, and the sky turned to the colour of a fading harebell, and the fire of seven different kinds of wood was kindled between the weapon-stone and the Chieftain's threshold, a quietness came over the waiting crowd, and men and women began to look towards the west, searching the fringes of the sunset for the first pale feather of the new moon.

Lubrin, searching with the rest, saw it at last, not even a feather as yet, but the white ghost of a feather, and knew that the time was come. All round him a faint murmur was spreading through the crowd. And in the same instant, from the women's court behind the hall there rose a high white shrilling of reed pipes, and below it the softer, darker crooning of women's voices making the Bride Song. And then all other sounds were engulfed in the booming of the sacred oxhorns that spoke with the voice of the gods.

And as the echoes died, there on the threshold of the hall stood Tigernann the Chief, with his priest-kind around him, Tigernann not in his man-self but in his god-self, his face covered by the god-mask with its towering crest of horsehair, on his wrists the sacred arm-rings that no mortal man might wear. Always at the greatest ceremonies it was so, the Chieftain ceasing to be a man to become something more, priest-chief, god-priest, god-chieftain, standing between his people and the Lords of Life and Death; and always at such times, awe and otherness came over the world and pressed upon the hearts of the people.

Again the oxhorns boomed, and with all the women of the dun behind her, Teleri came pacing from the

49

women's court. She walked straight and still and tall—taller, it seemed to Lubrin, than she had been yesterday—under the high moon head-dress with its swinging plates of silver that seemed too big and heavy for her slender neck. Perhaps it was the head-dress that made her look so tall. Perhaps it was the moon-marks chalk-painted on her forehead that made her look like a stranger . . .

Now Dara had stepped out from the Men's Side, and the two of them were standing before the masked figure on the threshold of the hall.

And the Chieftain's voice, hollow-sounding behind the god-mask, was asking the ritual questions.

"What things do you bring to the maiden, in place of those things which the maiden loses for you?"

And Dara made answer in the old, old words which came from the days when the tribe had been wandering hunters: "My hearth for her warmth, my kill for her food, my shield for her shelter, my spear for the harm that threatens her. These are the things that I bring to the maiden."

"They are enough," said the hollow voice behind the mask.

And Ishtoreth of the Oak came forward, carrying a great bronze wine-cup, with a dagger laid across the mouth of it. And Tigernann took the knife and made a small swift cut, first on the inside of Dara's wrist, and then on Teleri's, and let a few drops of blood from each fall into the wine—apple wine it would be, from the nine half-wild apple trees below the dun. It was always apple wine for a man-and-woman joining.

Then Dara and Teleri took the cup, their hands touching on its curved sides, according to the custom, and drank, and the thing was done.

Lubrin, watching them, the way they stood together, their hands on the cup, thought that though they had not chosen each other, all would be well between them, in a while, and tried to be glad.

Afterwards, the cooking-pits were opened, and, gathered about the Fire of Seven Woods, the whole dun feasted, the women carrying round the great jars of wine and barley-beer, through the firelight and the late summer dusk. And later still, when the full dark had come, they danced the Man-and-Woman Dance. They danced in two long lines facing each other in the beginning, advancing and retreating, slowly at first then faster and faster, to the high white shrilling of the pipes and the throb of wolfskin drums struck with fist and fingers and open palm. Then the two long lines became a snake, as, led by Dara and Teleri, each warrior caught the hand of the woman opposite to him, and peeled off, circling the fire; spinning sun-wise, faster and faster yet, shadows whirling out from them like vast black moths in the firelight. But suddenly Lubrin, dancing with a laughing red-haired girl from one of the outland settlements, thought that he felt another throbbing behind the rhythm of the drums. More urgent—desperately urgent—sweeping nearer, passing from sensation into sound. Others heard it almost in the same instant, and one by one the drums fell silent, and the dancers ceased their swaying and stamping, and stood as though they had taken root, every face turned in the direction of the one remaining gateway. Horse hooves on the summer-hard track, the broken rhythm of a horse near to foundering, yet sweeping nearer without any slackening of breakneck speed. Now the sound was on the causeway, plunging on through the gateway, out of the darkness into the flare of fire and torches. A rider on a spent horse, shouting his news before he reined to a stumbling and swaying halt, and dropped from the poor brute's back.

"The Attribates! The Attribates are on the war-trail—heading north!"

So the thing that the old men talked of had happened at last. And the night that had begun as a wedding feast ended as a ready-making for battle. Horses were rounded up and herded into the secret places of the Chalk and the forest for safety—to bring the herds into the dun was well enough in face of a raid, quickly come and quickly over; but in face of a long drawn-out attack the water stored in the rain pits would serve only for the people and the war-ponies and a few cattle for slaughter, and the rest must take their chance in the forest fastnesses, where there was water, and grazing of a kind. Chariots were being made ready, war-bannocks hurriedly baked; warriors sharpening sword and spear-blade on the tall black weapon-stone.

Twice more before dawn, scouts came up from the southern runs, with word of the enemy war-host—for it was a war-host, and no mere raiding party; three hundred chariots and more ran the word, beside the horsemen—heading for the great pass of the Downs westward. And once through that, all the northern runs would be open to the Attribates, and the great dun of the Iceni here on the High Chalk surrounded like a bear brought to bay.

Dawn came, unfurling mare's-tails of faint wind-cloud across the sky that was already beginning to shimmer with larksong; and while the shadows still lay long over every lift and hollow of the turf, the chariot teams were being led under their yokes, and the warriors standing ready to mount. And in the stable court, Lubrin Dhu, who had been out all night on the round-up, confronted his father, raging.

"Why?" he was demanding. "*Why* and *why* and *why*?"

"Because I give the order. Is that not enough?"

"Would it be enough for Brach or Corfil?"

The Chieftain was silent a moment, settling the great wolfskin cloak on his shoulders. Then he said, "Maybe not."

"Yet it should be enough for me? If I am not to go with the chariot column, *you shall tell me why*!"

One of the red ponies—Tigernann always drove a red team—jerked up its head, and side-flung into its yoke-mate; and the charioteer cursed softly in the background.

"Never you show your teeth to me, black puppy." The Chieftain brought his hands down in a sudden grip on Lubrin's shoulders, but his tone was not as harsh as his gripping fingers. "Listen, now, and understand. Dara, who will be Chieftain after me, must be beside me in the war-host, my sons also. Yet one son I must leave here with Drochmail who I leave in command, lest we fail and the dun be left to hold against these men from the south. Also lest, when we ride away, those we leave behind should feel already that we have abandoned them. Do you not see? They must have *one* of the Chieftain's sons with them."

53

"With the women and the boys and the old men," Lubrin said furiously.

"With the women and the boys and the old men; also with Drochmail, who is no better pleased than you, though he makes less yelping than you, being an older and a wiser hound."

But Lubrin was not listening to that part of what his father said. "And it must needs be me that stays? Because I am small and different from my brothers? Because I am the black puppy?"

"Not because you are the black puppy, but for a better reason than that—"

"I can ride, or handle a chariot, as well as Brach or Corfil!"

"*Hear me, I said!*" It was a sudden roar, and the grip tightened on his shoulders until the fingers bit to the bone. Then the Chieftain's voice grew quiet again, quieter than before; a voice only meant for the one hearer. "I have been patient, and I have no time for patience. I can trust Brach or Corfil, or Dara, to press home a chariot charge. For this, that may be a harder thing, I am not sure of them. But for this, I can trust *you*."

And under his father's gaze, the rage died in Lubrin Dhu. So—not for him the splendour and the rush and the shining of the chariot charge, with Dara beside him. For him, the slow waiting behind ramparts; no proud place among the warriors if his clan gained the victory, only the unsung bloodiness of the last stand, if it was defeat. He accepted what must be. "I hear you, my father," he said.

So the chariots rolled out through the great gate, the horsemen flanking them; the first level shafts of

the morning sun bright on iron blade and bronze har-
ness ornament, on the strings of Sinnoch's harp and
the tall crescent head-dress of Ishtoreth of the Oak;
for always the chief priest must be with the war-host,
to call down the strength of the gods, and the harper
to make a story-song of the battle that ends in victory.
The thunder of hooves and wheels died into the dis-
tance; and the white dust-cloud of late summer along
the Chalk rose behind them and swallowed them up.

And the dun was left to its waiting.

And standing on the rampart where it flanked the
great gateway, Lubrin saw inside his head how the
little knots of chariots and horsemen would be coming
in to join them as they went, by tracks and drove-ways
from lowland settlements and steadings in side-
valleys of the Chalk. Saw them strung across the
broad pass that was the way through for any war-host
from the south. Would the fighting come this even-
ing? he wondered, with the shadows of the chariots
spinning long across the land; or would the night
see watchfires all across the pass, and the fighting be
for tomorrow? How long to wait? And how would
the waiting end? His people were a small people, and
the Attribates a great one. Even if they had sent only
part of their fighting strength, there would be more,
and more, and more to follow up if need be; like the
cloud shadows drifting up on the south wind, and
always another scudding out of the blue distance
before the last one had passed over . . .

Beside him, old scarred Drochmail said harshly,
"Come. No good to stand here like two love-struck
girls mooning after the war-host. There is work to be
done, as well as waiting."

6

THE CONQUERORS AND
THE CONQUERED

There was work, and there was waiting enough, that
long day. In the early part of it, a few little bands from
the eastern runs came by, checked to shout for news
to the men on the ramparts, who had no more news to
give them, and then thrust on westward, to be lost in
the cloud of white summer dust. After that, no more.
All the warriors of the clan were gone to join the
hosting in the pass. And behind them in the dun, the
boys and the old men and the anxious-eyed women
went about their own grim preparations under
Drochmail's orders.

Food was cooked, for there might be no time for

cooking later; and the store cattle and few remaining horses were taken down the southern slope to the springs for the last time. After that there would be nothing for them, or for the human defenders of the dun, but the water in the rain-pits, as long as it lasted out. Lubrin and a handful of seventh-year boys from the Boys' House herded them down and back, for the Dark People, the Old People after the way of their kind, had melted into the landscape. Fighting among their overlords was no concern of theirs. Drochmail, shut-faced and dangerously quiet, saw to the issue of weapons. None of the women had gone with the war-host as the women of some tribes did, but they all knew how to handle a spear; and the boys swarmed up, fiercely joyful, to collect their slingstones and javelins; and as the day wore on, there began again to be a great sharpening of blades on the tall black weapon-stone in the Chieftain's forecourt.

There was a soft blustering wind from the south-westward all that day; and once, towards evening, they thought they heard the boom of warhorns far off. But though everyone checked in whatever they were doing, to listen with straining ears, there was nothing more to hear. Only the soughing of the wind along the curve of the ramparts, and the lowing of the few cattle penned in the berm between the inner and outer banks. But Lubrin took his sword back to the weapon-stone for another honing—whitt-whitt-whitt—as though the edge was not already as keen as honing could make it.

A girl stepped up behind him, and when he looked round he saw that it was Teleri, with the smudged remains of the moon pattern still white on her

57

forehead, though the tall silver head-dress had long since been laid aside, and her hair was knotted back with an old thong, to be out of her way. She gave him the spear she carried. "Make it sharp for me. Make it very sharp, Lubrin my brother." He had always thought her a soft little thing. But she showed her teeth like a young vixen.

"I will make it sharp enough to draw blood from the twilight," he said.

"So long as it will split the throat of a man!"

The night dragged by, and it was another day. And a while past noon there came the beat of horse's hooves along the track once more. But this time from the west. A single horse, hard pressed. And those who waited and watched in the dun swarmed to the ramparts to see who came—what came. They saw a single rider on a horse near to foundering, with another man, or the body of a man, slung before him across its withers.

People ran for the great timber gates, heaving them back just wide enough for horse and rider and bloody burden to pass through. The horse stumbled to a halt of its own accord, and stood with hanging head and distressfully heaving sides, while the rider half slid half tumbled from its back. And Lubrin, starting forward with a couple more, to lift down the man still hanging there, saw that it was his brother Corfil.

Corfil with his mouth open in a fixed grin not at all like his old wide scornful laughter, and the broken-off head of a javelin sticking out from between his ribs.

They lifted him clear and laid him down. All around, people were shouting questions. The horseman gave at the knees and sat down, his head in his hands. There was a great gash along his left forearm still oozing crimson, and his eyes were red-rimmed in the white dust that masked his face. "Water," he croaked. "Thirsty—"

Someone brought a cup, and it juddered against his teeth as he drank. "They're four to our one. They cut us to pieces."

"The Chieftain?"

"Dead. And Brach. Most of us."

Lubrin, with his brother's head on his knee, wanted to say, "Dara?" But he did not speak the question. It could make little difference now, anyway. They would all be dead soon enough.

"Get the gates barred again." Drochmail's voice cut through the rest. And to the rider he said, "How close behind you?"

The man shook his head. "Close enough."

And with the words scarcely out of him, they heard again, much closer this time, the boom of warhorns on the soft south-west wind.

So the fighting came. And when dusk rose in the hollows of the Downs, it was over. The dead lay sprawling in the broad ditches and across the ramparts, men, women and children. Attribates and Iceni spilled across each other, for Lubrin's people had not gone down tamely like cattle in time of sacrifice. And the kites and the ravens were circling lower in the sky. In the one remaining gateway, the dead lay thickest, where the Boys' House had fought their first and last fight; and the gates themselves were jagged mounds of charred and smouldering timber; the Attribates had set fire to captured chariots and sent the maddened teams against their own gates; and for all the spears of the defenders, some had got through, and there had been too little water to quench the blaze once it got a hold. And so after a time of blasting flame and screaming horses, the forefront of the enemy chariots had swept lurching and rocking in over the clotted masses of the dead.

Afterwards Lubrin remembered dimly some kind of last stand before the Chieftain's hall. Drochmail had been dead by then. He remembered stumbling over a body, and glancing down and seeing that it was the red-haired girl he had danced the Man-and-Woman Dance with, two nights ago. He remembered the breakthrough of enemy chariots, and the Attribates' terrible horse-skull standard with its blind eyes and streaming saffron tassels, rushing towards him, rearing over him like something in a nightmare. And then a thing like a jagged flash of lightning happening in the right side of his head.

After that there was a gap, not even darkness, just a piece lost out of time. And then, the world still swimming round him, he was standing with his hands bound behind his back—not sure how he came to be where he was, his head full of rags of half memories, of being a shadow penned somewhere among other shadows: of being kicked to his feet and dragged out of the penned place, of being sick. Unless it was all a dream. . . . No dream now. He was standing in his father's torchlit forecourt with bound hands, before a man who stood leaning somewhat wearily against the side of his reeking chariot.

The wheels of the chariot were juicy-red, and a

severed human head hung by its own bloodstained hair knotted to the chariot bow. He looked at it, and saw that it was his father's, and saluted it inside himself, ruefully. "I have done no better than Brach or Corfil would have done, after all, my father." He didn't seem to feel much, but after that first look, he was careful not to look again. He kept his gaze locked with the narrow blue gaze of the war chieftain. And he saw that it was the man he had ridden with at the autumn round-up, two years ago.

"I would not have shown you our horses, if I had known," he said dully, and shook his head to clear his eyes of the blood trickling from the half-dried gash on his temple.

"I am very sure that you would not." The fair man reached out and laid a finger on the slim bronze collar about Lubrin's neck. "You are the Chieftain's son? I bade them bring me a Chieftain's son, if one yet lived."

"This morning I was one of three," Lubrin said.

"And now?"

"Now I am the Chieftain's yet living son." And that was true. There had been a breath of life still in Corfil when they lifted him down from the foundered horse, but when they had drawn out the spear barb, the life had come too.

"So," said the war chieftain, "then you shall answer to me for your people, who I hold now between my hands. And when I would speak with them, you shall be the ears and the mouth between."

"And if I will not be the ears and the mouth between you and my people?"

"I am thinking that you will." The chieftain's

narrow blue gaze flashed open.

"Why will I?"

"Because you are their old Chief's son, the nearest thing to their Chief that your clan still have left to them; and always it is for the Chief to stand between his people and the gods. Between his people and Fate, we both know that, you and I."

And before Lubrin's inner eye rose the figure of his father standing here on the threshold of his hall, with the god-mask on his face, and the strangeness playing like summer lightning all about him. Yes, they both knew that, he and this war chief of the enemy.

So Lubrin Dhu took the weight of the chieftainship upon his shoulders, since it seemed that there was no one else left to take it.

And then his wrists had been loosed, and he was back in his penned place; seeing it now for what it was, the horse corral between the inner and outer banks, where the captives had been herded; seeing faces in the light of the guards' torches, black jagged figures half lost in the darkness between. The faces were turned towards him, and he searched among them for any that he knew; and found a few. A handful of warriors who must have been dragged back captive from the fighting in the pass; women, a few children. Others, stranger faces from the outland settlements, that he did not know, but were still the faces of his people. And on all of them the terrible stony look of defeat. Hardly any of the small desperate crowd seemed to be unwounded. Somewhere a man groaned, bubblingly, as though breathing his own blood. Somewhere a child was screaming, and a woman trying to hush it. On the edge of the torchlight, Teleri was kneeling over the body of a fallen man. The faint traces of the moon marks were still on her forehead; it was by that that her brother knew her.

The faces looked at him as though he was something that they had not thought to see again. They were asking questions in voices as numb as their eyes. Standing braced before them, Lubrin answered the questions. "Na, I am not wolf's meat. Not yet, none of us yet, I think. I have stood before their chieftain up in the forecourt, my father's head tied to his chariot bow. And I have listened, while he told me that when he would speak with you, who are in the hollow of his hands, he will speak through me, who am to be the ears and mouth between him and you."

He was aware of two winds blowing at the same time through the tattered remains of the clan before him. One was a kind of breath of relief. At least, that must mean there was to be no killing off of prisoners such as often followed such a victory. To die in battle was one thing, and not a great one, to a warrior people; to die as a sacrifice to the conqueror's gods was quite another. The other wind was a little cold one, and he did not in those first moments understand its meaning.

Teleri got up and faced him. There was blood all down the front of her tunic. "Why you?" she said.

Now that she had moved, the torchlight fell where her shadow had lain; and he saw that the man she had been kneeling over was Dara. Dara lying with eyes half open and half closed, a sodden mass of rags still oozing darkly between his neck and shoulder. He went closer, and stood looking down. "Will he live?"

63

"I do not know," Teleri said, and again asked her question, "Why you?"

"Because I am the Chieftain's son."

"Dara is the Chieftain."

And Lubrin, his head still too confused for clear thought, knew in the dark inmost places of himself that that was a truth better kept away from Dara, and from their captors, at least for the present time; better kept very far away indeed.

Mindful of the guards, he kept his voice down. "I am thinking that he will not make much showing as Chieftain, for a while and a while."

And Teleri answered as quietly, "I am thinking that he would not make much showing ever, as the ears and mouth between us and our conquerors!"

And Lubrin knew the meaning of the little cold wind.

The weight of the chieftainship was like to be greater even than he had thought.

The world had begun to swim round him again. By a great effort of will he kept himself upright on his feet, and walked away from her, away from Dara, into the darkest and farthest corner of the corral; and crumpled to his knees and began retching until it seemed that he must throw up the very heart out of his body.

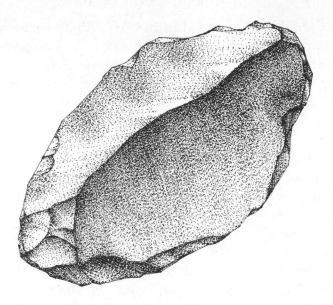

7
CAPTIVE WINTER

"What will they be keeping us for?" someone asked.

And "They will be having a use for us," someone answered. "We shall know it soon enough."

It was true that the conquerors had a use for them; and soon enough they knew what it was. Now that they had captured the dun, it seemed to the Attribates not large or strong enough for the frontier fortress of a great tribe. The turf and timber walls must be thrust out on the southern side, the remaining ramparts repaired and strengthened, the ditches dug wider and deeper. It was not for the Attribates, the Spear Lords, to do such work. It was work for the Old People, the Dark People. But the Old People had simply melted into the woods when the fighting began. One day, they would drift back, but not yet. That was always the way of the Old People, who saw the conquerors come and go or become Old People in their turn. So there was work and to spare, that autumn and winter, for Lubrin and the tattered remains of his clan.

At first, they were wild to rise against their conquerors and fight their way out.

Lubrin flung his whole weight against that. "It would be a fine red way to die, nothing more. Death for all that is left of the clan, even for the cubs. Have you forgotten the cubs? This way—"

"This way, we may live—with the Attribates' heels on our necks." Kuno, who had been with him in the Boys' House, looked him straight and bitter in the eye. "Easy it is to see that you have the Dark blood in you; easy it is to hear it speaking in your words."

And a jagged mutter of agreement rose around him.

A little drum began to beat deep down at the base of Lubrin's throat. He forced it into stillness. If they began to quarrel among themselves it would be the end indeed.

"He is of one blood with the Woman of the Clan!" That was Dara's voice, still not much more than a breathless croak, and looking round, Lubrin saw him, straining up on to his elbow from the old cowskin rug on which he lay in the shelter of the bank. His face looked as though it had been cut from the white inner layer of birch bark, his hair was still dark with sweat from the wound-fever that had scarcely left him. But his eyes, set back in bony hollows, were wide and challenging, and every hair seemed standing on end like angry hackles. "And if any man speaks such words again, let him wait until I can

66

stand upright, and I will thrust them back down his throat until he chokes on them!"

In that moment, Lubrin was sure for the first time that Dara was going to live. And there came to him the same rush of warmth and strength that he had felt beside the Chieftain's hearth on the night that Teleri was born. The warm sense of increase that comes in battle from the awareness of a friend's shoulder against one's own.

He turned again to face the rest of the clan. "In this way—" He took the thing up where he had left it, and found that now, angry and unwilling though they were, they were listening to him, and in silence. "If we hold together, and wait, as seed-time waits for harvest, one day our chance may come to be a free people once again."

"How?" someone demanded.

"I do not know." Lubrin heard his own voice speaking words that did not seem to be altogether his own. "I am not Ishtoreth of the Oak. If he were yet living, maybe he would know. It is in my mind that if we wait, surely the day will come when we are once again a free people. Maybe that also is the Dark blood speaking in my words."

The tongues of the Iceni and the Attribates were near enough kin for each to understand what the other said. But it had come to the Horse People almost from the first day of their captivity, that they could speak together so, even in the hearing of their guards, if they did not do it too often or too obviously, by using the tongue of the Boys' House. Every Boys' House made up its own tongue and spoke it during the training years, and then when the manhood rites

were over, never again. But now it was more impor-
tant to be able to speak together, without their con-
querors knowing every word they said, than it was to
obey the custom of the Boys' House. After a while,
they even let in the Women's Side, but that was not
yet.

Winter passed, and spring came back to the world,
and soon the swifts would be darting, sickle-winged
along the flanks of the High Chalk. Of the Iceni's
wounded, Dara and a handful more had mended, and
the rest had died, along with most of the old people
and some of the children. Some of the women had
gone too, but that was in another way, the old, old
way of women going to conquerors who have killed
their men. The Iceni saw them still, from a distance
among the women and children of the Attribates—for
the newcomers had brought up their own families
with them, as Lubrin's clan had done in their day, or
sent back for them before winter closed in. The Iceni
spoke the names of their dead, but they did not speak
the names of those women any more.

The work on the dun was well on towards its end;
the fresh-cut chalk of the ditches gleamed fiercely
white, the new wood of the stockades shone golden
where the weathered grey of the old timbers had
been. And a day came that started off like any other
day. . . .

Noon of that day came, and they laid down adzes
and antler picks, pots of lime-wash and the great
wicker carrying-creels, for the noon-time breathing
space. And Lubrin, in the broad flat bottom of the
outer ditch, saw a pointed flint lying loose beside his
left foot, and picked it up, for no reason except that it

was there, and sat turning it in his fingers and looking at it. On one side it was dark, almost blue, and flat; on the other it was weathered grey, and curved comfortably into the hollow of his hand. It had somehow not the feel of a natural flint, but of having been chipped out and shaped and used by someone, maybe very long ago; maybe long before the dun was there at all. He wondered who it was, and how his shaped flint came to be half-buried in the chalk. And while he wondered, a knot of horses went by at the gallop, along the turf below the dun. Down there in the ditch, he could not see them, but he heard the soft ragged flurry of hoofbeats sweeping nearer, and past, and dying away, and his inner eye, the eye in the darkness behind his forehead, knew the sight and shape and sweep of their passing.

The whiteness of the raw chalk was beside him, and the pointed flint was in his hand; and, almost unthinking, he began to draw on the wall of the ditch. It was the first time he had made a picture-magic since before the Attribates came. He drew the leading horse, and another half a length behind, and then a third. . . . He drew the speed and the power, and the blurred flow of manes and tails, and the thunder of hooves, and the restlessness of spring time in their heels.

A shadow fell across the white dazzle of the chalk, and he looked round to see Cradoc the Chieftain standing behind him. Cradoc, who had been last autumn's war-chief, and now was lord of the dun, often came striding along the new defences to see how the work went. He was standing with his legs straddled and his thumbs in his belt, his head tipped to one side. His narrowed gaze flicked from the scratches on the chalk to Lubrin's face and back again.

"What is this that you do?"

"I make a picture of the horse herd that went by just now," Lubrin said. "Did you not hear them?"

"I heard them." Cradoc looked more closely. "So-o. The leader I see. And this horse—and this—and then here is the last one of all. But what are these strange waving lines between?"

"That is the main mass of the herd."

"But they are horses—whole horses, as the others are?" Cradoc frowned, puzzled and enquiring.

"Surely. But you do not see them whole horses as the others are." Lubrin tried seriously to explain. "Unless you are watching a particular beast in their midst, when did you ever see more of a horse herd at the gallop than the first two or three, and the last one—and between, just the mass of the herd, that flows and changes as it goes?"

"I have not seen this kind of picture-making before," Cradoc said. "Do others of your people make in this way?"

Lubrin shook his head. "For my people, as for yours, horses are like the horses on the gold trading-pieces that you count for wealth. I draw what I see; but I think that all men do not see as I do."

8

THE BARGAIN

For a while, that was all. And then one evening
Cradoc grew bored in his hall after supper. He knew
all the songs that his harper could sing, and he wanted
something new. And he thought of the little dark
Chief's son who could catch the speed and power of a
galloping horse herd in a few flowing lines.

He crooked a finger for his armour bearer. "Ferra-
dach, go you down to the captives' corral, and bring
me up the old Chief's son; him they call Lubrin Dhu."

So a while later, Lubrin found himself standing in
the Chieftain's hall, where he had not stood since
before the Attribates came; standing before Cradoc
the Chieftain, who sprawled on the piled skins of the
High Place, where his father had sat and Dara should
have sat after him. He knew that if he looked up, he
would see his father's head, grinning and smoke-
withered on the roof-beam above him. He knew that

he should look up. But he could not force himself to look higher than Cradoc's face.

"Draw for me," Cradoc said.

Surprise made Lubrin check for a moment. Then he said, "Why will I draw for you?"

"Because I am minded for something new."

"Bid your harper to make a new song."

"He only makes the old songs over again," Cradoc complained. "Therefore draw for me—here on the hearth stone."

"I do not draw because another man bids me," Lubrin said.

The silence between them held while a man might take three breaths, slowly. ("They can kill me, but I will not make the picture-magic for them," Lubrin thought.)

And Cradoc answered the thought as though it had been spoken. "Na, na, it is not yourself that I shall kill. But let you remember that you answer to me for your people."

The sickness rose in Lubrin's throat; but he remembered the tattered remains of a clan, who were his people; and he asked between his teeth, "What would you have me draw?"

"Draw more horses," said Cradoc the Chieftain.

So Lubrin took charred sticks from the fire, and squatted down beside the hearth-stone, and began to draw. It was the same stone on which he had tried to draw old Sinnoch's harpsong, so long ago.

He drew a pair of fighting stallions in a few swirling and savage lines, while the Chieftain leaned forward, arms across his knees, and the warriors and their women crowded close to look. And then he rubbed

72

the lines away, and drew a mare giving suck to her foal. And then he drew a war-pony standing at check, head up to listen to the sound of distant warhorns, or maybe snuffing the wind for the scent of danger to the herd. But when he would have rubbed that away also, the Chieftain leaned forward quickly and caught his wrist. "Na! Let be!"

So Lubrin laid aside the charred stick, and sat back on his heels. And while he squatted there, waiting like a hound, he thought, for his master's whistle, and while all about him, the warriors looked on, Cradoc continued to lean forward on his crossed arms and stare down at the war-pony scratched in its few char-wood lines on the hearth-stone. In a while, he held out his hand for his great bronze wine-cup, and when his cup-bearer brought it to him, took it and drank deeply, then sat up and looked round at his crowding hearth companions. "I have been thinking."

"Cradoc the Chieftain has been thinking! Sound it forth on the warhorns!" said Anbar, who was the Chief's foster-brother, and free to jest with him as not even the rest of the hearth companions quite dared to do.

Cradoc's teeth showed, strong and crooked in the flash of a grin, but he shook his head. "I have been thinking it is a sore waste of horses, this making on the hearth-stone and then brushing away almost as swiftly as though they were formed of the hearth smoke itself. I have been thinking that now we have carried our frontiers up here onto the High Chalk, and made our new rampart of the old run of the Downs, and pitched our outmost herding tents here in this dun that we have made greater as befits a great people—"

("That *you* have made greater!" thought Lubrin, feeling the scarred hardness of his hands, and remembering old men and sick men who had died among the timber and wet chalk in the winter that was past.)

"—and surely it would be a fine thing if, here on the outward-facing scarp, we should have such a horse as this one, but half a hillside high, cut into the chalk, to last for all time and say to all men that here stands the frontier of the Attribates." Cradoc brought both hands down with an open-palmed thwack on his knees. "To say that here stands our landmark, not to be shifted while grass grows over the Chalk and foaling time returns with the spring!"

One of his companions nodded. "Such a horse of power would give its strength to the frontier. Also it would please Lugh the Sun Lord, that he may send us many foals and many sons."

"That, too," said an older man, sagely. "Aye, surely such a great Sun Horse, which is the sign of the Attribates, his people, must find favour with the Sun Lord!"

The talk washed to and fro over Lubrin's head; and then Cradoc was speaking to him again. "Have you the skill? Could you make a horse the like of that?"

A horse cut out of the downland turf, white against the green, half a hillside high. Lubrin could see it. And from somewhere a memory came to him; a very small memory, of lying out along the branch of his wych-elm and holding up a leaf and finding that he could make it cover his father's dun and its whole hillside. Maybe one could begin the horse like that. Make a first drawing very small, and hold it up and notice where the lines came? "I do not know," he said. "A horse that size is surely a task for giants; but there might be a way."

"So. The new walls are all but finished. Let you take as many of your people as you need, to help you."

"There are none that I shall need," said Lubrin, and got to his feet.

"To clear so much turf yourself would be a task for a giant indeed. You will need other hands beside your own."

"You have it wrong. I shall not need my people's help, because I will not make you your hill-high Sun Horse," Lubrin said flatly. "I think that there might be a way, but I will not seek to find it."

Yet again there was a waiting silence, Lubrin and the Chieftain staring levelly at each other, and the warriors watching to see what would break between them.

"It is not wise to speak such words to me," the Chieftain said at last. "You have shown me already that you do not fear what I can do to you. But I have told you already to remember your people, who lie in the hollow of my hand." And as he spoke, he slowly clenched his hand into a fist, tighter and tighter until the knuckles shone yellow-white and it seemed as though blood might come oozing out, dark as crushed bramble juice, between the fingers. It was a gesture that said more than words could do.

And the silence settled again, thick as a swarm of flies.

Then, looking his conqueror eye into eye, Lubrin said, "Such a thing as this horse you speak of cannot be made unwillingly. If you force me, by threats of what you will do to my people, I can try to make the thing for you. But the gods will not breathe life into it at another man's commanding; and what I make will be without power or meaning as an unlit lamp. You may have your horse, but it will not be worth having."

And even while he spoke, he was aware of the silence continuing inside himself; and in the heart of the silence, something telling him what he had to do. He was aware of other things too, at the same time; the saddest and most surprising of them, that there could so easily have been friendship between him and the fair-haired man in the High Seat, who he was fighting for the life of the clan. And again, he was aware of the blackened and withered head on the roof-beam. He wrenched up his own head as though to meet its dead gaze, and cried out to it in his heart, "Tigernann my father, you said it might be a harder thing than to lead a chariot charge. I do what I may to save the clan; that is more important than all else. It is the only thing that matters now."

Then he lowered his eyes to meet the narrow blue gaze of the living man. "Cradoc, Chieftain of our conquerors, I will try to make you your hill-high Sun Horse. I will make it willingly—for a price."

Cradoc raised his brows. "Lubrin, Chieftain's son of our conquered, what price is that?"

"If I succeed, you shall let those who are left of my people go free. You shall let them have enough stallions and brood mares out of the herd to raise a new herd in another place." ("Good grazing, in and out between the hazel woods and the heather," said the merchant's voice in his mind, across the years between.) "And you shall let them go."

"It is a high price that you ask," said Cradoc.

76

"But you only pay it if the Sun Horse seems to you good."

"There is truth in that," said the Chieftain, staring into the heart of his wine-cup. Abruptly, he looked up. "So, then, that shall be the way of it. The new ramparts, I have said it before, are all but finished; and already the Old People are beginning to creep back after the way of their kind. If the Sun Horse seems to me good, it shall be for your people's freedom. That is the bargain between you and me. . . . I have had enough of horse pictures for one night."

And so Lubrin Dhu left the Chieftain's hall.

And all the while, he knew that there was something more; something that had not been spoken between them, not even thought between them; but was still there, in the dark heart of things; waiting.

Later that night, in the corral between the inner and outer banks of the dun, Lubrin Dhu gathered the rags of the clan about him, to tell them what had passed beside the Chieftain's hearth. But looking round from one to another of the faces turned towards him in the mingled light of the cooking-fire and the rising moon, he found it hard to begin; harder even than he had expected, and he had not expected it to be easy.

Kuno asked, "Well then, Ears-and-Mouth of the Chief, what thing did he want with you?"

"He wanted me to draw horses for him on the hearth-stone, to amuse him because he grew weary of his harper's song. And when I had drawn him as many horses as he wanted, he bade me say could I make him a Sun Horse, cut into the turf of the

77

northern scarp. A horse half a hillside high, to be a frontier mark for the Attribates."

"And you said?"

"I said that I did not know. I said it was in my mind there might be a way—for one that was willing to find it."

"And you were willing?" someone said.

Kuno leaned forward into the firelight, "Are you telling us that he asked this of you, and you refused, and yet come back to us with your bowels still in your belly and your head on your shoulders? That is a story hard to swallow."

"Na," Lubrin said, slowly. "I did not refuse, I said that I would try—at a price."

Teleri his sister cut him short, her face a hard white mask in the growing moonlight. "You should find the task easy enough, for you will be able to copy the horse from one of the gold coins they use. I am thinking it will be in gold coins that they pay you?" Her voice matched her face, hard and coldly accusing. And the silence of the rest seemed to accuse him also.

"The tails of those horses are wrong," Lubrin heard himself saying, as though it mattered. "Our horses have their tails set on in a different way."

"But it will be *their* horse that you are making."

"It will be their horse, the Sun Horse of the Attribates, yes. But it will be the Moon Horse also, the horse of our people, so that so long as the Downs rise above the forest, and men make their prayer to Epona the Mother of Foals, they will know that the Iceni were here."

Below in the woods, an owl cried mockingly in the silence; and the silence was cold as the moonlight.

78

Lubrin felt the chill of it, and knew that they thought, all of them, like Teleri, that he had broken faith with them. And for a moment anger and grief rose in him so that he could not find words to set the thing straight.

It was Dara who broke the silence and the chill. "This price that you speak of—I think that it is not in gold horse-pieces. Let you tell us what it is, Lubrin, my brother."

"Aye," a score of voices took up the demand. "Let you tell us what it is!"

"I said to the Chieftain that I would try to make him his Sun Horse half a hillside high; and that if I brought it to finish, and it seemed to him good, then what was left of us, of the clan, should go free, taking enough stallions and brood mares from the herd to raise up a new horse herd in other runs than these."

A low murmur rose from the listeners. And Dara said, "So-o! *That* is a price indeed!"

And someone else spoke up from the dark behind him. "But will he keep his share of the bargain? It would be easy to say, when the horse is finished, that it does not seem good to him."

"Cradoc will keep his share of the bargain," Lubrin said. "And I shall keep mine." His gaze found and held Dara's. And between them again, unspoken, was the old shared dream of the northward droving. Once, he and Dara had thought to share that leadership together; and then, when Dara had been named at the Choosing Feast, to marry with Teleri and be the next Chieftain of the clan, Lubrin had known that if ever the dream were to become more than a dream, it would be for him to take the leadership alone. And now the thing was the other way over. Now it would be for Dara to lead the people north, while he. . . .

For an instant, the thing that he had been aware of in the Chieftain's hall, the thing that had been left unsaid, unthought, began to stir. He thrust it back into the dark, not looking at it. The time for looking at it was not yet. "I shall need help," he said, "hands to cut turf and carry chalk."

"You shall have them." Dara held out his own in a gesture of offering, as he said it.

And Kuno added, "We've had practice enough, by now."

And Teleri came forward from among the women, and reached out with a quick shy gesture that did not quite touch his wrist. "I will carry chalk for you. Let you forgive me, I did not understand."

But the loneliness, that had begun for Lubrin on the first night of their captivity, had deepened, and did not go away.

9
OF HAWKS AND GODS
AND MEN ON THE GROUND

Next day Lubrin went down from the dun, past the
nine sacred apple trees that were swelling into bud,
and away through the valley woods to the wych-elm
on the edge of its clearing. He was alone. He had been
surprised at first that Cradoc had not ordered at least
a couple of men with spears to go with him; but then
he had understood. Cradoc knew as well as he did
that there was no need; he could not run, while his
people were still captive in the dun.

The great tree was smoky with tiny purplish
flower-tufts, and the scent of it, and the boom of bees
were all about him as he climbed. And all about him

too, as though it had been waiting for him, the old sense of shelter and home-coming. He climbed up by the familiar road, swinging his way from branch to branch until he was clear of the tops of the lesser woodshore trees; up and up until he was lying out along his special branch, with all the broad lowland stretch and the distant wave-lift of the Downs rising to his father's dun clear before him.

It was all as familiar as part of himself, but now he was looking at it as he had never quite looked at it before; seeing the long slow masses of the hills that seemed to rise with the sunrise, and travel westward to set far, far off with the setting sun. Even the sudden lift where the land reared up above plunging combes and hollows, carrying the dun on its highest crest, did not break the line. It was as though the High Chalk arched its neck as it passed on westward, no more.

"Now," said the Youngest Son, "let us take the
   horse herds, high crested and of fiery heart,
And let us set our faces toward the West,
Toward the land of the trees of silver apples.
   Come."

The words and the beat of Sinnoch's harpsong feathered across the back of his mind. He pulled round the deerskin bag he carried behind his shoulder, and took out the pieces of silvery birch bark and the charred sticks wrapped in a bit of old cloth. His eyes were full of the long-familiar rise and fall of the skyline, the changing play of light over the lifts and hollows. Below the dun and a little to the left, a small flat-topped hill rose from the lower slopes of the Downs—there was an old tale of a dragon that slept, coiled up within it, guarding a magic spear—and behind it, already taking on the clear green of spring-time, the north scarp of the Chalk swooped upward to the skyline. Somewhere below that skyline, he thought, would be the right place for his horse.

He began to draw on his bits of birch bark. He drew again the horse that he had drawn on the Chieftain's hearth-stone, standing tensed and alert, head up to snuff the wind; a war-pony hearing the sound of distant warhorns, a stallion on guard over his herd. That was the right kind of horse for a frontier mark.

All day he lay out along his branch, making his drawings and gazing at the hillside, until hillside and horse came together in his mind's eye, and he knew just where the lines must run, from that thorn-tree to the lip of that hollow; and down in a flat curve towards the loop of the old drove-way. He made it all into a kind of pattern on his last piece of birch bark; and then, with the shadows lying long in the evening light, he dropped out of his tree and made his way back to the dun.

And when the dusk had deepened into the dark, and the evening meal had been eaten in the Chieftain's hall and corral where his captives were penned, Lubrin Dhu stood again before Cradoc the Chieftain in his High Place. "I have been all the day seeing how the lines must run, and now I know, and I am ready to begin the horse. Therefore give me leave to fell birch saplings in the valley woods tomorrow, and lime that is left over from whitening the rampart timbers, and ten oxhides. And let me take who I will from among my own people, to help me, and in two days I will set out the first lines on the slope above the Dragon Hill."

"And by means of a few oxhides and saplings and some lime daub, you will take these lines from inside your own head and make them again on the hillside?" The Chieftain frowned, interested and perplexed. "How shall such a thing be done?"

Lubrin shook his head. "Let that lie for a while. I have not done this thing before; nor do I know of any man who has done it. Therefore I must learn the secret as I go along; and until I have learned it—I cannot tell."

"So, that is fair," said the Chieftain. "Not tomorrow but in maybe three days' time, when the defences of the new gates are finished, you shall have your oxhides and your lime, and leave to fell your birch saplings, and any that you choose from among your own people to work for you."

So three days later, Lubrin and Dara, and the other men who had come forward to join them, went down to the valley woods to cut the birch saplings, and toiled back with them up the snaking track, their spear-guards following watchful on either side. It seemed that with almost the whole Men's Side out, Cradoc was less sure of them than he was of Lubrin alone. It took them the best part of two days to cut and carry all that they needed, and get it stacked up just below the Ridgeway, as near as the hill slopes allowed to Lubrin's chosen place. After that was done, they trimmed the oxhides and daubed them with lime so that they would show up from a distance, white on the young green of the turf. And then Lubrin was ready to begin.

It was a blustery day when they started setting out

the oxhides to serve as markers, brow and muzzle, neck, flanks, breast and tail, and the four firm-set feet; and the wind, gusting up from the west through the spring grass and the white-fleeced thorn trees, scattered the larksong all about the sky and drove clouds of lime-dust from the flapping oxhides into their faces, so that their eyes smarted and grew red-rimmed. Lubrin shouted his orders to Dara and the rest. "Over that way towards the second thorn tree. Let you try forty paces—na, na, you are working too far uphill. Kuno, hold it there, while I go to the left— Dara, help me get this one pegged down . . ."

Otherwise they did not speak. There seemed nothing to say.

Lubrin felt strange and un-belonging on the familiar hillside, and he could catch none of the feeling of magic that was a part of his picture-making. There was no more life or magic in what he was doing now than there had been in digging out the new ditches for the dun. Instead, there was an oddly dead feeling. Maybe it was because the work was so big that he could not see what he was doing. He had never drawn anything before, without being able to see in the same heart-beat as he set them down, whether or not the lines were what he wanted them to be.

When he could get away far enough to see what he had made on the hillside, it would be all right, and the life and the magic would come.

But by the time they had all the hides in place, and pegged down or weighted with lumps of chalk to keep them from flapping out of true, the wind was blowing up a fine mizzle rain that smudged away the lowland woods behind drifting swathes of wetness. So it was not until next morning, when the rain had cleared and the larks were singing over the High Chalk, that Lubrin dropped down from the dun and headed across the valley for his usual vantage point. And all the way, he was careful not to look back; not until he came to the right place.

He had been anxious lest the wet night should have washed away too much of the lime-daub, and the oxhides not show up well enough from the distance. But when at last, far out on his branch, he parted the twig-tangle and looked, there they were, easy enough to trace in the clear light of early morning after rain.

He lay for a long while studying marker after marker, thinking out the white lines of the bared chalk that should join one to another, linking muzzle to ears, forming the single sweep of neck and back and tail, running from the forelegs up the arch of the neck to the head once more. It would be a good horse. Some of the markers, he thought, were not quite in the right place; one needed to be moved nearly twice its length to the right, another should go about the same distance farther up the hill. He thought so; but it was so hard to be sure, with the slope of the hillside running away from him. High over the vale, a buzzard was swinging in sky-wide circles, the tips of its broad flight pinions tilted by the lift of the upper air. Its faint mewing cry came down to him, and watching it, he thought that if only he could see as the great bird could see, circling up there against the shining steeps of the sky, with the broad upward thrust of the Downs slowly circling beneath him, he might know. ... No, there would be no help in that; the horse must be seen always by men on the ground. No man

86

could ever see from up there; only the buzzard and his kind, and maybe the gods. It was all so confusing that it hurt his head as well as his heart. Only one thing he was sure about: those two markers needed shifting. He would do the best he could, being a man and not a god.

Wearily he dropped down out of the wych-elm, and set off yet again, back towards the dun and the conqueror, and the tattered band of fellow captives who were his people.

CHIEF'S RIGHT

In the days that followed, they daubed the birch stems also with lime, and set about laying them from one to another of the marker points, driving in tent-pegs to hold them from rolling away down the scarp, then gathered up the hides and set them aside to serve their purpose again at the next stage. And now the outline of the horse was clear on the hillside. Not that you could tell it for a horse; not that you could tell it for anything but a maze of lime-daubed saplings lying at random on the turf, as though giants had been playing some kind of game with them.

"This is a *horse*?" Dara said doubtfully, rubbing

88

the back of one hand across his forehead and leaving a white smear of lime-wash.

"If we were far enough away to see it," said Lubrin, and looked up at the buzzard still wheeling and mewing against the evening sky, with the late sunlight under its wings. "To him—I think—it will be a horse."

"But we have not his wings."

"Na. But from across the vale, too. Today, the light is too far gone; but tomorrow's morning I shall go to my tree, and then I shall know if it is a horse."

That night, lying huddled in an old cloak, he watched the stars wheel overhead until the sky paled to grey, and the first faint primrose feathering of dawn grew in the east; and never slept at all, knowing that the coming day was going to be one of those that change life, or begin it, or end it, or make it grow.

Morning came, the woods below the dun ringing with birdsong; and Lubrin drank the morning buttermilk when the women brought it round, but left his piece of barley bannock untouched, and went to the thornbush gate of the corral. The others watched him go. He could feel them watching between his shoulder-blades. Dara half moved as though wanting to come with him. But he was alone as he passed out from the corral, and alone as he came to the gate of the dun, and the spear-guards passed him through.

And so, alone, he went out to his wych-elm, and climbed to his special branch, and looked across the level land and up the slopes of the Chalk, to see whether the thing that he had outlined up there in whitened birch poles held in it the beginnings of a horse, or not.

Yes, it was a horse, sure enough, legs and tail and all where they should be; the head maybe a little small, but that could be easily made bigger. You could see at once that it was a horse, not a bull or a hound. And yet it was all wrong. Standing there, legs down and head up, it made a kind of break in the lovely sunrise-to-sunset flow of the Downs, pulling the eye up short. Sudden as a sword-gash, he thought. A sword-gash—a kind of death. . . . Yes, that was it, the horse was dead, the outer shape of a horse, but empty of the life that should be in it. It was just as he had felt it, battling with the lime-daubed oxhides up there on the windy hillside.

He lay still on his branch a long time, wondering what he should do now, while the light of the spring morning changed around him, and the fine mesh of shadows from the budding elm twigs swayed and shifted, and still the buzzard swung mewing in its sky-wide circles above the vale. He thought that Cradoc and the rest of the Attribates, maybe even most of his own people, would not see as he saw. In all likelihood he could just go on, and cut his horse into the chalk, and no one would ever know that there was anything wrong with it. But he would know. He would know that he had not kept his part of the bargain in full. He would know that he had betrayed his own kind of seeing. And it would be an ill thing to know that of the last picture that he would ever make.

The last picture.

In the splinter of time while the knowledge was only a half-knowledge within him, the buzzard sighted its prey and came plummeting out of the sky and, away over towards the foot of the Downs, something died. Too far for Lubrin to hear any cry, if there was one, but he was sharply aware of the small death as though it had happened in his cupped hands.

In that split moment of time, the unspoken, unthought thing between him and Cradoc came out of the dark, and he looked it in the face, and found that he had always known it. It was the last sealing of the bargain between them. It was his own death. His blood, his life to quicken the god-horse of his making; just as the Old People shed the life of a man into the furrows every seven years to quicken the seed-corn to harvest.

He found that his hands were clenched and shaking, and his heart racing as though he had been running hard on the hunting trail, and there was a churning sickness in his belly. Carefully he unclenched his hands and watched them grow steady as though he was watching somebody else's. The sickness passed and little by little his heart quietened. Lying out there along the branch, he accepted that he was going to die for the rags of his clan. There was nothing strange in that, after all. It was the king's right, the Chief's right, to stand between the people and the gods; to die for the people when the need came. That had always been the way of it. He was all that was left of the Chief's sons, and the horse was of his making. But he needed a little while to grow used to his accepting, before he went back and looked again into the faces of other men. He needed the strength and the quietness of the great tree. And slowly, the quiet came to him; such quietness that after a while he even slept a little, having lain wakeful all the night before.

And the old dream of the white mare that he had not dreamed for a long time, came back to him. His sleep was so light that it was almost a waking dream, and there was a moment when he roused from it, when dream and waking overlapped, and he saw the white mare and the distant hillside with the same eyes. Then the dream faded, and left him to the waking world. But he had seen the two together, he had seen the horse, the mare, that he must make up there on the high scarp of the Chalk. He knew how she must move, flowing with the flow of the Downs on their way from sunrise to sunset. It was as though Epona herself had touched him in his sleep, saying, "See—this is the way that it must go."

The shadows were growing long as he dropped from his tree, and yet again started on the way back. This time he did not make straight for the dun, but swung away eastward, climbing uphill by the dizzying slope behind the Dragon Hill, out onto the high emptiness of turf where the dead patterns of birch saplings waited for him. He did not know quite why he went there. There was nothing more that he could do that evening; but the place called him, and he answered the call. And then, as he stood there thinking of the new lines that he would begin to set out tomorrow, he heard horses' hooves behind him on the turf, and turned, half expecting a mare as white as thorn blossom. But it was Cradoc, riding his favourite red stallion, with a couple of hunting dogs loping along behind.

The horse had been one of Tigernann's, and was surefooted as a goat on the plunging slope. Cradoc reined him in, and sat looking down at Lubrin, and from him to the birch saplings, the wind plucking at his saffron cloak.

"Strange," he said, "up here it means nothing at all, but from across the vale it begins to be a horse indeed. The work goes well."

And looking up into the bright, harshly blue eyes of the man above him, Lubrin knew that he had been right. He could finish this horse, if he wanted to, and nobody but he would ever know that he had not kept his bargain to the full. Nobody but he would ever know that he had betrayed the dream, the vision that comes to all the makers of the world, before they make a new thing, whether it be a song, or a sword, or a chalk-cut horse, half a hillside high.

He shook his head. "It does not go well. There is no life in it, and it is the wrong horse. But I know now how to make the right one, and tomorrow I will start again."

"And if I say that this horse pleases me well enough?"

"It must also please *me*," Lubrin said. Suddenly he smiled. "So. We struck a bargain, that I should make the horse, and if it seemed to you good, my people should go free. But if this is the last picture-magic that ever I shall make, let me make it to the best that is in me."

There was a small sharp silence. The red stallion flung up his head and side-stepped on the steep turf, as though his rider had jerked the rein.

"Or is it that you think I only seek to gain time?" Lubrin said. "A little more time to go on living? That would be a sad way to die."

And the thing was out in the open between them.

93

Cradoc shook his head; and something in his face told Lubrin that for him, too, the thing had been left lying in the dark, until the moment came for looking at it.

"When the horse is finished, and seems good to both of us, I shall be ready," Lubrin said.

High over the Chalk, the larks were singing, the shimmer of their song tossed to and fro on the evening wind. Cradoc said, "The priests have not demanded it."

"The priests have no need." Lubrin put up a hand to thrust back the dark hair that was blowing in his eyes. "They know that the thing is for the chief-kind. They know that it is in the pattern between you and me; and between the people and the gods."

II

THE GREAT LONELINESS

When Lubrin went back to the corral the dusk was
deepening and the light of the cooking-fires beginning
to bite. Faces turned questioningly towards him, and
Dara looked up from the strap that he was mending,
and asked, "Is it well with the White Horse?"

"Na," Lubrin said, "it is not well, though Cradoc
sees nothing amiss."

"Surely that is all that matters," said Teleri, from
the Women's Side.

"Na," Lubrin said again. "It is not all that
matters." He looked round at the faces in the firelight;
the faces of his people; seeing them very clearly and

very completely, now that he knew he was going to die for them.

"What more?" demanded Teleri, fiercely, as though suddenly she was trying to deny something.

"It matters that it should be worthy of Epona, the Mother of Foals," said Lubrin Dhu. "And since my life will be shed to quicken it when the making is finished, it matters that it should be worth dying for."

A rustle of sound not much louder than a caught breath rose from the small tattered crowd, a stirring of little movements quickly stilled. But there was nothing startled in their stirring. They too, knew the pattern.

Only, out of the quiet that followed, Dara looked up from the strap that he was working on, and said, "I am the new Chief. It should be for me to die for the life of the clan."

"Na," Lubrin said, "it is for you, who are the new Chief, for you and for Teleri to lead the clan north to the new herding runs. I am the old Chief's son, I am the maker of the horse. Epona herself has shown me the way that it must be done. The dying is for me."

It was all quite simple now, as complete and inevitable and rounded in on itself as the way a white convolvulus flower opens in the morning and when the single day of its life is over, folds back at evening into the shape of the bud.

He sat down beside Dara. "Tomorrow we will start the work again."

So they began the work again, laying the lime-daubed hides and then the saplings. And Lubrin went to and fro between the hill scarp and his

96

look-out tree. But now it seemed that Epona had indeed touched him, and he could not put a line wrong. Now, it was not the outer seeming of a horse that he was tracing up there on the steep hillside, but something far closer to those picture-magics in which he had tried to catch the pattern of a swallow's flight or the struck notes of a harp.

One long, lovely, unbroken line swept the whole length of arched neck and back and streaming tail, more than a hundred and twenty strides from pricked ears to tail-tip; yet at its broadest place, the light belly was little more than four strides across. The head had something of a falcon's look about it; the two farthest legs did not join the body at all. None of that mattered. He was not making the outward seeming, up there among the drifting cloud-shadows and the lark song. He was making the power and the beauty and the potency of a horse, of Epona herself, though his conquerors would never know it.

Dara and the rest said nothing as to the strangeness of what they did. But they were too close to see more than the scatter of markers on the grass, and maybe they did not know it, and would not know it until the day they set out on the northward drove, and looked back from across the valley. They did what Lubrin told them to do, as they would have carried out the bidding of the priest-kind, as the oxhides were replaced once again by the lime-daubed saplings, and the rough outline of the saplings was followed out more finely with long strips of pegged hide—even one oxhide cut round and round can make a good broad strip more than a spear-throw long. And all the while, they took care, even Teleri, even Dara, never to step in his shadow. His sun shadow or his moon shadow, or even his shadow cast by the cooking-fires in the corral at dusk. And he began to feel very much alone; even more alone than he had done before, and in a different way.

On the evening that the pegged outline was complete, Lubrin Dhu walked the whole length of it, starting from the muzzle and returning to the muzzle again. No use now to go out to the wych-elm, the slender lines of the rawhide strips would not carry so far on the sight. But the feel of the turf beneath his feet as he went told him that all was well.

"Tomorrow we will start cutting the turf," he said to Dara, who had walked with him at a little distance.

"So much hurry?" said Dara, with a rawness sounding at the back of his throat.

Lubrin was looking into the west, where a long flight of feathery cloud was touched to flame by the setting sun. "It is not only the turf we shall have to cut away, but all the top chalk until we come to the clean white underneath. It will take a long time, and it may be that things will happen to hold us back. The weather may break. And all must be finished by harvest, or it will be too late to start north this year. We must make good time while we can."

So the next morning they began to cut and lift the turf. Lubrin himself made the outside cuts with a bronze axehead, while Dara and the other men stripped away the green hide of downland turf with its starring of small bright flowers, clover and thyme and eyebright, to be carried away by the women in their great creels and tipped into the deep, bush-grown hollow far below.

Days went by, and days went by, and the men with their mattocks and broad deer-horn picks were digging down into the chalk itself; cutting away the dull earth-stained top layers for the women to carry away and stack in spoil-heaps; then into the clean white chalk thigh-deep beneath the grass. And that, too, was stacked nearby, ready to go back on top when all the duller surface chalk had been shovelled in again.

And all that summer, as the huge strange figure took shape on the hillside, and men a day's journey away saw it on their southern skyline, and wondered what magic the men of the High Chalk were making, all that summer, the weather was gentle, so that the barley grew tall-stemmed and heavy in the ear, in the corn plots along the flanks of the Downs, with no high winds or thunder rain to beat it down. And the brood mares dropped strong foals; so that men knew the magic was good, and in after years spoke of that time to their great grandsons as the Summer of the White Horse.

The work drew on towards its end, and the corn ripened to harvest; and on the day that the last swathe was cut, Lubrin Dhu smoothed the last layer of white chalk on the strange bird-horse head, and knew that his work was done.

Next morning, while his own clan and those of the Old People who had returned, were gathering in the sheaves, he went out to his looking-tree. The branches of the great wych-elm that had been purple-flushed with early spring-time when he began the work, were deep-layered now with the broad dark leaves of summer's end. And he had to pull aside two branches to make an opening, before he could look across the vale and see the thing that he had made.

There she was, the white mare of his dream, moving at an easy canter, as though she knew that she had far to go; her arched neck and the long streaming line of her tail echoing the sweep of the Downs, as though they had been part of each other since the morning-time of the world, and would be part of each other while time lasted. He saw how strange she was, with that almost falcon head, her two furthest legs that did not even join her body. But he saw that it was her strangeness that gave her her lovely lightness of movement, that made her a creature of fire and moonlight and power and beauty. And looking out to her through his gap in the branches, Lubrin knew that he had come as near to catching the wholeness of the dream, as near to making a perfect thing as it is given to mortal man to do, even when the finger of his god is upon him.

Now there was only the one thing more that he had to do.

He laid his hand against the rough bark of the wych-elm, as though touching a friend in farewell, knowing that he would never feel the liveness of the great branch under him again. Then he dropped to the ground, and for the last time of all, headed back towards the wave-lift of the downs, and the dun that had been the strong-place of his clan, to tell Cradoc of the Attribates that he was ready.

He found the Chieftain in the stable court, looking at a new chariot, the swallows twittering under the eaves and darting low among the midge cloud overhead.

"Cradoc the Chieftain, I have made you your White Horse, your frontier-mark. Will you go now, and look?"

Cradoc looked up from examining the rawhide lashings of the yoke-pole, and shook his head. "I have watched it in the making, as I came and went all summer long; that you know well. There is no need that I go now and look."

"Then let you say—does it seem to you good?"

"The first horse would have seemed as good," Cradoc said. "But we are both of a Horse People, you and I." (Memory tugged at Lubrin: his father in that same court saying much the same words. The swallows had been darting low that time, too.) "We know a fine mare when we see one. She will bring many foals to the horse herd, and fine sons to the Women's Side. Yes, she seems to me good."

"Then I will go and bid my people to make ready for the drove," Lubrin said.

"In four days, it will be the feast of Lammas. When the Lammas fires are cold, the horses shall be ready, and the gates stand open for your people to go free," said Cradoc the Chieftain.

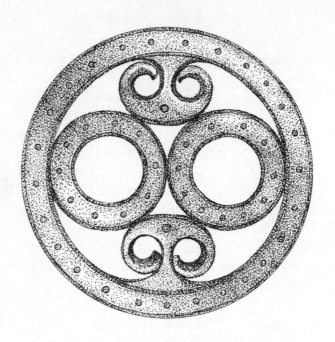

12

SONG OF THE
NORTHWARD DROVING

The horses were brought up, trampling through a cloud of white summer dust, and corralled close to the dun. A small mixed herd, not the flower of the horse-runs, Lubrin saw, looking them over, not the dregs either; Cradoc was playing fair. Two stallions penned by themselves, one dark brown, one fox-red, a score or more of mares, several of them showing signs of being in foal; a scatter of rough-coated two-year-olds, who would likely give trouble on the journey, five herd ponies. . . .

On Lammas Eve the twin fires flared on the high ridge of the Chalk eastward of the dun, and the pick of the cattle and horse herds were driven between them, that they might be fruitful in the coming year. They came up out of the dark, with a soft thunder of hooves, the herdsmen shouting behind them. And Lubrin, standing among his own people—for they too, were gathered to the Lammas fires—saw it all, as he had seen it so many times before; the wild-eyed high-crested stallions, the frightened mares with their foals at heel, bursting out of the dark into the red glare of the fires, then gone again into the dark, over the crest of the ridge. Once he glimpsed among the torrent of up-flung heads and streaming manes and tails the gleam of firelight on a milky flank, as a white mare went by, out of the dark and into the dark again like a dissolving dream. Like the white dream-mare who had been a part of him all his life, and now waited for him, cut into the chalk only a spear's throw below the crest where the Lammas fires streamed out on the light wind.

Last of all the horses, the fox-red stallion and the three best of his mares went through between the fires, that they too, should have the year's fruitfulness to carry north with them. And when the cattle had followed, and the fires were sinking, some of the young warriors began to catch their women by the hand and run with them through the last dying flames, so that they might have fine sons. Dara stepped forward from the gaunt and ragged Men's Side of the Iceni and caught Teleri by the hand, and ran with her, their feet scattering the glowing embers, and she skirling like a springtime curlew in the sudden sharp gladness of coming freedom. Others of the Iceni followed. They would need bairns as well as foals in the new herding runs.

Lubrin watched them.

Now that the flames had sunk little and low, no more than curled petals of fire here and there among the ash, the night sky that had been blotted out by the red flare of them had come back, and with it the stars; the stars of wayfaring and the hunting trail and the herding runs. Lubrin was glad that it was a night of stars.

Morning came, with the green plover calling, and a faint mist that lay low across the forest until it grew ragged and wisped away before the sun. And the white mare on the hillside gazed back open-eyed into the morning sky. And the great gates of the dun stood open for the people of the Iceni to pass through. Three of the men who were to ride herd had already mounted; and the little band of horses had been brought from the corral. Goods and small children were being loaded on to a couple of ancient war-carts or into panniers across the backs of small sturdy ponies; men and women carrying creels and bundles, one leading an elderly goat. Some of the men were carrying spears for the first time in many moons; the women had their tattered and weather-stained gowns hitched high through their belts for wayfaring. There were no old people. The year of captivity had taken a heavy toll of the old, because they were without hope; some had even drunk sleeping-juice as the time drew near, knowing that they must be left behind or become a burden to the rest of the clan.

Not like this had been the droving of which Sinnoch the Harper had sung, thought Lubrin Dhu; the chariots making their wheel-thunder along the High Chalk, the spreading horse herds, the ox-carts for the women and children, the goods and gear, the bellowing of driven beef on the hoof. Yet perhaps this was more valiant, this handful of warriors and women worn to the bone with captivity, setting out with nothing but a kind of threadbare hope. . . .

The round solemn eyes of a child met his over the rim of a pony-pannier; a gaunt dog sniffed at his heels, then padded off after its master. Soon, now, they would all be gone. They looked at him standing there in the opening of the great timber gates; but there was little, almost nothing, that they could say to each other.

At the last moment, Teleri came to him, brushing back from her forehead the fair wisps of hair that were escaping as they had always done, from her thick braids. She did not look like a girl at all. Her bones, he saw suddenly, were beautiful, and sharp, so sharp you felt you could cut your hand on them; and her eyes seemed already full of long distances, even while she looked into his face.

"May you come safe to the new horse-runs," he said, seeing that she did not know what to say.

She made a little movement towards him, then drew her hands back, without touching him at all. "We shall come to them," she said, with clear certainty, "and we shall not forget that that is your doing. Maybe one of the little ones in the war-carts has already the gift of harpsong in him; maybe the gift is waiting for one not yet born. If that is the way of it, I hope that he will be born to Dara and to me. But one way or another way, the time will come, in the horse-runs in the north, when the clan will have

a harper again, and he will make a song of the north-
ward droving, which shall be also the song of Lubrin
Dhu.''

Again she made the little movement, and again
drew back, not touching him, and turned away.

It was a long time since anyone had touched
Lubrin, or eaten from the same bowl. That had begun
at the same time as they had begun to avoid stepping
in his shadow and the great loneliness had come.

And soon, so soon now, they would all be gone.

And then, on the very edge of their going, Dara,
who had been making a great thing of seeing to all the
last-minute arrangements, so that Lubrin thought he
would go without any leave-taking at all—well, he
would like enough have done the same thing if they
two had stood in each other's places—Dara flung
down the bundle of rugs that he had been loading
on to one of the ponies, and came back into the gate-
way and put his arms round Lubrin's shoulders,
daring whatever taboo he might be breaking with a
courage made reckless by grief.

For a breath of time, Lubrin stood rigid as the new
timber of the gate pillar. Then he flung his arms
round Dara, who had been heart-friend and more
than brother to him since they were five years old.
For one long moment they strained close, each driving
his face down into the hard hollow of the other's neck.

''Heart-brother,'' Dara said, ''wait for me in the
Land of Apple Trees. Whether it be tomorrow, or
when I am lord of many spears in the north, and too
old to sit a horse or lift a sword, wait for me until I
come. And do not be forgetting me, for I will not for-
get you.''

"I will not be forgetting," Lubrin said.

And they parted touch, and Dara turned away to the herd pony which one of the other men was holding for him nearby. He mounted, and flung up his hand in the signal to be off. Horses pricked forward under the slap of their drivers, and the wheels of the two old wagons began to turn; men and women hitched up bundles; the herd-riders set the herd on the move. Somewhere among them a child began to cry, thinly, like a newborn lamb.

Lubrin turned and went up to the northern rampart to watch them away.

He saw the ragged skein of men and women, the two old war-wagons that looked as though they would not hold together beyond the first day; the meagre horse-herd and its drovers out to one side; seen and lost and seen again, as the track looped, sinuous as a whiplash, among the steeply falling combes and headlands of the Downs, until they gained the valley floor, and crossed the ancient Road of the Horse People and headed out along the northward track. Somewhere, he knew, they would look back, and see the great white mare on the hillside; and then they would not look back again, but keep their faces to the north, following the dream of the distant grazing lands between the mountains and the sea.

There were so few of them, less than two hundred to the youngest child. He wondered how many more would be born on the way, how many would die. How long it would take them to get to the place where they were going. A year? Two years? Half a lifetime? He wondered if they would ever get there at all.

The white dust was rising behind them, and the track ran into the trees.

He watched until he could not see even the dust-cloud any more.

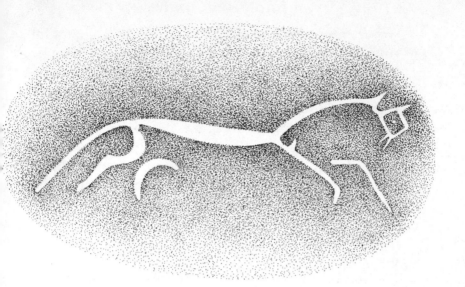

13

SUN HORSE, MOON HORSE

Before noon the people were gathering, the new lords
of the High Chalk streaming out from the dun to
freckle the hillside more and more thickly with their
blue and brown and saffron and poppy-red. Even at
midday, on the steep northward-facing slope, the
shadows of man and bush and hummock and hollow
spilled out long and thin like the shadows of evening.
But after the long hot summer the turf was bleached
pale and tawny, and the smell of sun-warm grass and
small aromatic downland flowers that beat up from it
was unmistakably the scent of high noon. Lubrin
smelled it above the thicker, musky smell of the
crowd, as he stepped out into the clear space around
his great chalk-cut mare. A little wind carried with it
the cool shadow-scent of trees up from the valley

woods over the bare shoulders of the Chalk, and he
smelled that, too, and heard the sharp cry of a kestrel
hanging high overhead. The crowd was very quiet, so
quiet that there was nothing to blur the bright harsh
splinter of sound. A faint blue heat-haze lay over the
low country. He had known it all before, as long as he
had known life; but he had never been so sharply and
achingly aware of it. It was as though there was one
skin less between himself and the wind and the sun-
warm turf and the kestrel crying.

He was naked, his body painted with red and yellow
ochre, in patterns that were not the patterns of his
own people; and the priests had set lines of dark berry
juice on his forehead and about his eyes. Two of the
priest-kind were on either side of him as he walked;
and on the turf between the mare's forelegs, two men
waited for him. One was Cradoc, clad in his cere-
monial mantle of blood-red wool fringed with mar-
tens' tails. The other was the High Priest, swaddled
in cloth that was bleached white as only the priests
might wear it, crowned with oak and yew; fat like an
acorn-fed hog, in the way of the priests of the Attri-
bates, who lived too richly on the offerings to the
gods; and holding a knife of some darkly polished
blue-green stone.

Lubrin saw the knife; and it seemed as much a part
of him as the wind and the warm turf and the sound
of the kestrel crying. But he did not wish to take his
death from the hands of this stranger-priest. That
had not been in the bargain.

He looked at Cradoc. "This is a thing between you
and me."

"Assuredly, this is a thing between you and me,"

Cradoc returned. "Among my people there can be no god-ceremony if the priest-kind do not give it their presence. But this is a thing for the chief-kind, my brother."

And he held out his hands to the High Priest beside him, and the man laid the strange dark knife across his palms.

Side by side, Lubrin and Cradoc stepped onto the bare white chalk of the mare's breast. A low rhythmic murmur rose from the gathered priests, and was taken up by the crowd, rising louder and louder, becoming prayer and triumph-song in one. The mare's arched neck was like a royal road, and Lubrin walked up it like a king going to his king-making. He came to the strange half-falcon head, and it seemed to him that the proudly-open eye stared back at the sun and moon and circling stars and the winds of all the world. "It is only a round patch of turf, after all," said something within him, laughing gently at his own foolishness. But something else, deeper within him, knew that it was strong magic, the touch-spot where earth and sky came together; and something else said, "There is a harebell growing on it. That is the most wonderful thing of all."

Then he lay down.

"Are you ready?" Cradoc said, kneeling beside him.

Lubrin smiled up into the narrowed blue eyes in the wind-burned face. "I am ready."

He knew the high wind-stippled sky above him, and the warm steadfastness of the ground beneath. He knew the harebell growing in the tawny grass, tossing on its thread-slender stem as the wind came by. From somewhere far away in time and place, he knew the weary joy of his people's homecoming to their herding runs between northern mountains and the sea.

"Brother, go free," said Cradoc.

He saw the sun-flash on the descending blade.